For all who wish for greater control over th
own matters better while interfering wi.. ...

"For whoever keeps the whole law and yet stumbles at just one point is
guilty of breaking it all." James 2:10.

Table of Contents

Foreword

Your Story

My first client at the start of my law career well over two-and-a-half decades ago was only a little more than half my age and education but nonetheless at least twice so wise as me. He knew that if he could get alongside a decent lawyer and maybe an accountant, real estate agent, banker, and one or two other solid professionals, then with all of his energy and ambition, his life and business would soon take off. I had little clue yet of the value of law services when clients fully embrace the power, authority, and purpose of the law within a vital and ambitious life. My teenage client owned one ancient piece of business equipment for which he still owed the kindly seller who had foolishly extended him credit. Yet with the professional help that he so consistently sought and accepted, he was before long so soundly organized, authorized, positioned, managed, planned, prepared, financed, and insured, and so well respected by his friends, competitors, and even his few enemies, that he became a resounding personal, family, financial, and business success. My first client knew and respected the authority of law to guide a business and life. My hope is that you do, too. Let this writing be your tool.

1 Are You Legal?

Your Audit

This program encourages you to audit your legal rights, responsibilities, and opportunities in each significant area of your life so that you can take charge of your flourishing. Law is all about empowerment. This program is your total-empowerment tool, your legal audit for better control, risk management, peace of mind, and prosperity. An audit is simply an examination against standards. Financial audits help businesses, nonprofits, and governments account for the proper application of funds. Businesses also perform legal audits, although less formally and regularly than they do financial audits. This program brings the legal audit to you as an individual. Businesses have a lot at stake, which is why they undergo regular audits. You have no less at stake, relatively speaking, than they do. You have no excuse for disorderly conduct, financial affairs, employment and family relationships, or properties, leaving legal risks you have no need to face. Your life has value to you and others. Examine it through law's lens. Experience and enjoy the power of lawful purpose. Answer for yourself the question, "Are you legal?" not just so that you can avoid punishment, liability, or other penalty or sanction but to improve your life and the lives of those around you.

Your Rights

Americans live under the rule of law, and thank God for that. Think of it: have you ever had to do something because of the whim of someone else that you did not want to do? Probably not. In societies without the rule of law, citizens must marry, move, take jobs, change jobs, avoid or abort their second child, cover their heads, not vote, not drive, not offend the government, not start businesses, and do or not do any number of other important things, against their will and at the whim of their rulers. You, though, as an American, have the rights and protections of the rule of law. Because you live in America, you act within a bubble of protections against unreasonable interference by others, especially by the government. The rule of law is not perfect here. It takes constant work on the parts of many simply to keep it as relatively strong as it is. Yet because you live and act within these precious protections, you stand the greatest chance of making something of your life, even as others around you do likewise.

Your Responsibilities

With rights come responsibilities. Even in America, you must do certain things, not because of the whim of others but because responsibilities are a part of rights. Because you have the right to liberty, you must respect the liberty of others. Because you have the right to property, you must respect the property of others. Because you have the liberty to contract with others, you have the responsibility of keeping your promises. Because you have the right of public protections and facilities, you have the responsibility to pay public taxes. Because you have the right to marry, you have the responsibility to care for your spouse. Because you have the right to procreate, you have the responsibility to care for your children. Because you have the right to recover loss due to the carelessness of others, you have the responsibility to insure or pay for the harm your own carelessness

4

causes others. Every right has a corollary responsibility. The rule of law pursues and preserves both equal rights and equal responsibilities.

Your Opportunities

Yet the rule of law is not simply about rights and responsibilities. The rule of law is at its core about opportunities. The rule of law is about the opportunity that we each have to flourish. The rule of law does not entitle us to flourishing. Flourishing takes insight, wisdom, virtue, discipline, and effort. The rule of law instead guarantees that we can reap the reward of our insight, discipline, capability, productivity, and effort. Americans often do not fully appreciate their opportunity to flourish within the rule of law. Because the rule of law is our birthright as Americans, we often ignore our opportunities as much as we overlook or disrespect our rights and responsibilities. Americans are by and large no more virtuous, smart, or energetic than people elsewhere. Yet for all of the opportunity that the rule of law creates for us, we should be more of a lot of good things that we are not. We should be so good, wise, and engaged, making everything of every opportunity, because the opportunities that the rule of law create are so precious.

Your Power

Your opportunity is exactly what this workbook addresses. The premise of this workbook is that if you fully appreciate and vigorously pursue your rights, responsibilities, and opportunities under the rule of law, then you will prosper to a far greater extent than if you live in ignorance of that power. The rule of law has the power not simply to protect you from the invasions of others while keeping you from interfering with others. The rule of law is not simply a negative injunction. Rather, the rule of law is a positive guide to your greatest opportunities. The rule of law helps you manage risk not simply to reduce negative consequences but to increase positive consequences. Nothing ventured, nothing gained. We commit ourselves to so many activities and projects. Each time we do so, we risk things, whether time, money, relationships, or other attributes, conditions, and resources. The rule of law helps us manage those risks into the best consequences. We tend to pursue self-improvement by therapeutic, psychological, physical, and cosmetic means, when law has a power of its own, often far more specific, clear, and practical, to contribute to our well-being.

Your Scorecard

Those areas of your life to audit begin with your personal conduct. You should comport yourself with respect for others. Law will have something to say to you if you do not. Yet the quality of your personal comportment also presents important opportunities. The same is true for your education that you should know and pursue your educational rights, responsibilities, and opportunities. The law provides you access to education and favors your saving and borrowing for it while requiring that you repay educational loans. Likewise, the law has much to say about how to save for, rent, buy, maintain, pay for, and sell housing. The law address how you purchase, operate, sell, and use vehicles for transportation. The law addresses how you apply for, gain, benefit from, get paid for, and leave employment. The law addresses your rights, responsibilities, and opportunities within your family, with your finances and taxes, and in your business and missions. The law also secures you important freedoms of which you should be taking full advantage. Complete this audit in each of these areas, and watch your life improve. For each subsection where you see the **Score [___]** indication, give yourself a score 1 through 5 as follows:

1 My legal affairs here are so seriously out of order that I am suffering serious losses and facing profound uncertainty in this area, negatively affecting me, my family, and those around me. I need help putting those affairs in order and plan to take prompt action.

2 My legal affairs here are largely unattended even if not seriously disordered, when attention is clearly due now. They expose me, my family, and those around me to significant risk that could at any time lead to serious loss if not addressed as I now plan, as others well know.

3 My legal affairs here are in basic order as things now stand but would not do in the event of likely developments. While attention to them does not appear to be an immediate need, I am missing important opportunities to order and improve my life, which I hope to soon do.

4 My legal affairs here are in good order for now and in the event of foreseeable developments. While they leave me and my family peace of mind and need no apparent attention, I nonetheless suspect that with review and counsel, I could make them work even better.

5 My legal affairs here are of no concern whatsoever. I have so effectively addressed, managed, and ordered them that they contribute substantially to my well-being and the well-being of my family and those around me, even to the point of being my legacy.

2 Your Conduct

Get a hold of yourself! The integrity of your personal conduct toward others is a critical part of your legal audit. Nothing and no one else can save you—not a rich uncle, political connections, great luck, insanity plea, magical superpowers, or liability insurance—if you are not consistently thinking and acting right. If your personal conduct violates law, rule, regulation, or community norm, then you need to modify that behavior now before the consequences catch up with you. Read and respond to each of the following sections to ensure that your personal conduct is meeting the requirements of the law. You may think that you do not need to consider one or more of the following sections on crimes, criminal history, fraud, and negligence, but we all need to pay attention to these things. None of us is immune from the law or from the vices and temptations that bring us into conflict with it.

Your Crime

Do not underestimate the risk of committing a criminal wrong. Few people graduate from high school or college with prison as their goal. Yet crime is a problem at every income level and in every demographic, trade, or profession, not just among the poor or undereducated but for everyone. Individuals of middle or high income, education, and reputation still commit the most grievous criminal wrongs including murder, rape, and child abuse. Many more commit criminal wrongs involving illicit drugs, solicitation for prostitution, embezzlement, conversion, forgery, mail-and-wire fraud, retail fraud (shoplifting), uttering and publishing (bad checks), stalking, and similar lesser crimes that nonetheless seriously and permanently impact their careers, relationships, and reputations. If you are involved in or contemplating criminal activity, then stop immediately no matter your belief in whether law enforcement will detect it. Assume that law enforcement knows everything that you know. Do nothing criminal, ever. You have plenty to do otherwise. Keep it legal.

Audit: Do you agree that otherwise decent people sometimes commit surprising wrongs with serious consequences, so that we should all be careful to respect the law? If you disagree, then consider these examples: O.J. Simpson (football, television, and movie star incurs multimillion dollar civil judgment for double homicide); Bill Clinton (U.S. president impeached for perjury and obstruction and disbarred); Jeffrey Skilling (Enron CEO convicted of multiple felonies); Bernie Madoff (investment advisor convicted of multibillion-dollar fraud). **Score [___]**

Available law services: responding to requests for criminal investigation; defense of criminal charges; consultation on criminal laws; expungement of criminal record.

Your Record

If you have no criminal record, then remember to keep it that way. Do not plead guilty to crimes that you did not commit. If you are considering pleading to a crime you did commit, then first investigate with your lawyer the diversion, deferred-conviction, delayed-sentence, and other programs to improve your record or keep it clean. If you have a criminal record, then consider expunging that record. Depending on your state's law, you may be able to expunge one conviction if it is your only conviction and five years have passed since the conclusion of any sentence. Expunging a criminal record means completing a court process to remove it from your record. Doing so can restore rights and privileges having to do with public assistance, housing, employment, licensure, voting, weapons, and other matters. If your conviction does not qualify for expunging, then know that law-reform movements in some places are modifying some of the harsher effects of conviction. For example, ban-the-box movements have led to some state and local laws prohibiting employers from requiring job candidates to disclose convictions on job applications. Employers may still confirm and consider criminal histories when doing background checks, for convictions that indicate unfitness for the work.

Audit: If you have no criminal history, then confirm your intent to keep it that way. If you have a criminal history, then obtain a copy of it, review it for accuracy, and confer with a lawyer to determine whether you may expunge it. Act now, whether you need to or not, to assure future opportunities. Score [___]

Available law services: responding to requests for criminal investigation; defense of criminal charges; consultation on criminal laws; expungement of criminal record.

You as Accomplice

Others judge us by the company we keep. You need not be actually committing a crime for authorities to hold you

11

responsible for acting as an accomplice to the crime or participating in a criminal conspiracy. Accomplice and conspiracy convictions require that authorities prove more than your mere presence in the vicinity of criminal activity. Yet authorities may draw accomplice and conspiracy evidence from acts that you might have assumed were innocent. You have other reasons not to consort with others who are committing crimes. Authorities may mistakenly conclude that you were responsible for the crime. Those who were responsible may even give false testimony blaming you. Authorities may attempt to hold you criminally responsible for illicit drugs, open intoxicants, illegal weapons, child pornography, and other evidence recovered from your vehicle, home, clothing, computer, or other property even if you did not put that evidence there and were not aware of it. Do not keep company with others who involve themselves in illegal activities.

Audit: Identify in your mind any acquaintance of yours whom you believe engages in criminal activity. Commit to not interacting with that person when that criminal activity may be ongoing and to not allowing that person access to your property that the person could use for that criminal activity. **Score [___]**

Available law services: responding to requests for criminal investigation; defense of criminal charges; consultation on criminal laws; expungement.

You as Victim

While you may not commit a crime, you might on the other hand become the unfortunate victim of crime. Promptly report to police any suspected personal or property crimes against you. Your ability to prove the crime later, whether for punishing the wrongdoer, recovering insurance, or avoiding your own responsibility or liability, often depends on prompt report. Take reasonable steps not to encourage crime. Do not leave your keys in your vehicle. Close garage and house doors when you are away. Leave a light on if you are out for an evening. Lock doors at night. Get a co-worker to accompany you to your parked vehicle when in the dark. Have your vehicle keys in hand and ready to unlock your vehicle before you get to the vehicle in the parking lot. Without being unnecessarily fearful, just be aware that people commit crimes particularly when most convenient or provoked, and practice habits to discourage and avoid both. If the unfortunate happens, then know that state laws provide crime victims with certain rights. Those rights may include notice of charges and dispositions, opportunity for hearing, orders of restitution, and partial recovery from crime-victim funds.

Audit: Identify from among the following examples the three most likely crimes that others might commit against you, identifying for each the action most likely to discourage the crime: (a) larceny from your unlocked residence; (b) larceny from your locked residence while away one evening; (c) theft from your unlocked vehicle; (d) theft of visible items within your locked vehicle; (e) theft of your idling vehicle outside the coffee shop; (f) theft of your smartphone left at your workstation; (g) robbery walking alone to your parked vehicle late one night at the far perimeter of the mall parking lot; (h) identity theft using your password 123456; (i) assault by a drunken fan with whom you argued at the ballgame; (j) felonious assault by an angry commuter who shot your tires out after you cut him off to get ahead in line at the McDonald's drive-through. **Score [___]**

13

Available law services: identity-theft protection; representation for restitution; preparation of crime-victim-impact statements; application to crime-victims fund.

Your Offenses

Some conduct, while not necessarily criminal, nonetheless crosses the line into dignitary offenses for which the law would hold the wrongdoer civilly liable to pay damages to the victim. Do not underestimate the law's sensitivity in this area. Sharp disagreements, major or minor feuds, and petty disputes can cause us to act out of character and uncivilly toward others. While we might have no actual intent to harm another, actions that make another think that we are about to cause an offensive contact, like brandishing a weapon, can qualify as civil assault. Gossip that hurts another's reputation can qualify as defamation. Looking through another's papers or things can qualify as invasion of privacy. Following or attempting to encounter or confront another person may qualify as stalking. You may have good reason to suspect, investigate, and even punish neighbors, co-workers, and others, but the law strongly disfavors personal retribution. If you have a beef against someone, then take it to them first, and if not satisfied with their response, then to your lawyer. Do not engage in self-help actions that could subject you to civil liability. Leave others alone. Mind your own business, or get a lawyer's help in minding the business of others.

Audit: Identify which of the following may present potential liability issues for you, where you may be interfering with others: (a) physical fights or altercations with others; (b) threats or suggestions of violence toward others; (c) unwanted sexual advances toward others; (d) sexual jokes and innuendo around others in the workplace; (e) things that you have said or

14

done that prevent another from getting a job; (f) interfering with another's business causing them loss; (g) prying into another's personal affairs; (h) snooping into another's personal papers, effects, journals, diaries, or computer files; (i) gossiping about others in ways that harm their reputation; (j) running down the reputation of others; (k) posting offensive notes, slurs, symbols, or insults on social media or other publicly accessible location; (l) tailing, following, or otherwise pursuing another person to observe or confront them. Can you think of any other liability risks you face for personal offenses against others? **Score [___]**

Available law services: evaluating potential civil claims against others; representing you in those claims; obtaining, challenging, or modifying personal-protection orders; evaluating potential civil claims against you; defending you in those claims; evaluating insurance coverage to protect you; invoking insurance coverage for claims made against you; suing insurers for liability coverage.

Your Fraud

You probably would never think that you or any other decent person would engage in anything close to fraudulent conduct. Unfortunately, otherwise decent individuals do commit frauds of various kinds with surprising frequency. The problem is partly that people do not know what fraud is and partly that people naturally want to do a little better for themselves in any transaction than they ought. Non-lawyers do understand that fraud is basically a scheme, scam, or swindle—activities in which decent individuals would never engage. What you may not realize is that the law's definition of fraud includes any intentional misrepresentation causing another to rely to their loss. Small omissions or exaggerations

15

that may seem to you to be harmless can nonetheless be fraudulent. For example, when a vehicle owner applies for motor-vehicle insurance omitting to disclose requested moving violations, the owner defrauds the insurance company of a higher premium and would lose the insurance when the insurer discovered the omission. When the seller of a home conceals and falsely denies a roof or basement leak, or the seller of a motor vehicle actively conceals a need for repair, the sellers defraud the buyers out of price breaks. Be scrupulously honest whenever dealing with any person or business. Do not operate under a detection (will they catch me?) standard. Be open and up front with what you know. The civil remedies for fraud can be substantial. Some states even recognize civil liability for careless and innocent misrepresentations.

Audit: Identify which of the following may present potential claims against you for fraud, involving your recent sale of a defective, damaged, or misrepresented: (a) vehicle; (b) bicycle; (c) motorcycle; (d) camper or trailer; (e) home; (f) piece of home equipment; (g) computer; (h) smartphone; (i) other piece of consumer electronics; (j) consumer service offering; (k) time share or rental; (l) business; or (m) franchise or business opportunity. Can you think of other transactions in which you have been involved as either a buyer or seller in which you may have misrepresented or concealed conditions or circumstances? If so, then consult with a lawyer regarding the steps to take to correct those circumstances including resolving your liability. **Score [____]**

Available law services: reviewing the terms and conditions of a proposed transaction; providing documentation of "as is" sales; completing a seller's disclosure statement; conducting due diligence for a transaction; helping you respond to due-diligence requests by others; evaluating fraud liability and claims against you; evaluating your fraud claims against others; reviewing with you insurance, mortgage, other loan, employment, and other application forms you intend to complete to ensure accurate and complete disclosures.

Your Negligence

The greatest legal risk that most of us face is not that we will commit a deliberate crime or offense harming another but that we will hurt someone or damage something valuable by acting carelessly. The law calls damage-causing carelessness *negligence* while providing that the careless wrongdoer pay for the harm through civil liability in negligence. The most-common example involves motor-vehicle accidents. We are all at one time or another careless when driving, one hopes not too often and not causing any accident. When motor-vehicle accidents happen due to driver negligence, and the accident causes serious injury to another, the driver and vehicle owner may well have negligence liability (depending on state law, and given that some states limit negligence claims under no-fault acts — see more about motor-vehicle accidents under the Transportation section of this book). Civil liability in negligence also exists in some cases for damage due to other careless acts whether in maintaining buildings and lands, engaging in social and recreational activities, selling goods and services, and even in the workplace. You should not be careless in what you do, especially when your activities create unreasonable risks of personal injury or property loss to others.

Audit: Identify which of the following activities you are directing or conducting that may be creating unreasonable risks of personal injury or property loss to others: (a) operating power tools around others; (b) making power tools available to others; (c) storing or using explosive, combustible, or toxic materials; (d) providing daycare or other supervision for children not your own; (e) maintaining a pool, trampoline, swingset, or other recreational improvement available to others; (f) involving others in water

17

sports using your equipment or direction; (g) storing or using firearms; (h) operating a home-based business selling goods or services to the public. For each activity that you identified or other risk-creating activity that you direct or conduct, evaluate whether the activity is reasonably safe. In each instance where you identify unreasonable dangers that may exist, consult your lawyer regarding actions you should take to address your potential liability before it arises. **Score [___]**

Available law services: evaluating the risk of potential negligence claims against you for specific activities; drafting releases of potential negligence claims, that you request from others to participate in activities with you; representing and defending you against negligence claims; negotiating settlements of your negligence liability; drafting releases of your negligence liability after settling claims against you; evaluating your potential negligence claims against others; negotiating settlements of your negligence claims against others; representing you in pursuing your negligence claims against others; reviewing releases of claims presented to you in settlement of your claims.

Your Insurance

You have another way to manage responsibly the risks of your own misconduct, in addition to being reasonably careful in what you do. You should also be insuring risks. Insurance is simply a way of transferring the risk from you to the company that insures you. As a general rule, you should be insuring risks that you cannot afford if they occur, for which you can afford the insurance premium, and that are reasonably likely to occur. We address life insurance, health insurance, disability insurance, property insurance, and vehicle-damage insurance in other sections of this book. Here, though, consider again the risk of your injuring others or damaging the property of others because of your negligent or other wrongful conduct.

18

Liability insurance of different kinds covers some of those risks. For instance, if you purchase homeowner's insurance to pay for the repair of your home in the event of a fire, that insurance also routinely carries a liability coverage. If you hurt someone doing something carelessly, then your homeowner's insurance may, depending on the circumstances, provide coverage up to its liability limits. If you are on a nonprofit board, then the nonprofit may have liability insurance to cover your board liability. For any activity in which you engage that carries risk of loss, consult with your lawyer and insurance agent about available insurance coverage. Insurance policies have limits and exclusions that make professional evaluation wise.

Audit: Describe the scope of coverage (your activities that these policies insure) for each of the following liability insurance policies you or others have in place for you covering your liability to others: (a) motor-vehicle liability insurance; (b) homeowner's insurance; (c) directors-and-officers (D&O) insurance; (d) errors-and-omissions (E&O) insurance; (e) malpractice insurance; (f) commercial general liability (CGL) insurance; (g) products-liability insurance; (h) umbrella insurance. Do you think you may need any of these liability insurances put in place? **Score [___]**

Available law services: evaluating liability-insurance needs; evaluating liability-insurance limits; evaluating liability-insurance coverage; evaluating liability-insurance exclusions; invoking liability insurance coverage to defend and indemnify you against negligence claims; suing liability insurers for coverage to defend and indemnify you against negligence claims; evaluating bad-faith claims against liability insurers refusing to settle claims against you; suing liability insurers for bad faith in refusing to settle claims against you.

Your Substances

Law addresses alcohol and substance abuse in a variety of ways. Alcohol is so frequently involved in serious motor-vehicle accidents, domestic violence, and other careless and violent acts that it bears separate treatment. State laws make driving under the influence of alcohol a serious crime for which the convicted can go to jail or prison, lose their driver's license, and lose their professional license and job. State laws also prohibit serving alcohol to visibly intoxicated persons or minors. State laws also hold bars and other places that serve alcohol (known as *dram shops*) civilly liable for injuries or deaths caused by patrons whom they serve alcohol while visibly intoxicated or minor patrons whom they serve alcohol. Some states extend that dram-shop liability to social hosts who serve alcohol to minor or drunken guests. In other words, you may have to pay if you serve alcohol to minor or drunken guests who then seriously injure or kill another in a vehicle crash or violent act. Alcohol is not the only abused substance. Individuals abuse prescription drugs, illicit drugs like cocaine, designer drugs like methamphetamine, and even glues, fuels, and other household substances. Do not underestimate the prevalence of substance abuse and the losses it causes. More people now die in the U.S. from poisoning usually associated with drug abuse than from motor-vehicle accidents. You could face criminal charge for delivering abused substances to adults or minors, or civil liability to persons whom they harm. Take special care not to abuse alcohol or other substances and not to allow others to do so using substances under your control.

Audit: Identify in which of the following activities you sometimes engage or stand risk of engaging: (a) driving under the influence of alcohol or other substance; (b) serving alcohol to another person who then drives under its influence; (c) making alcohol available to minors; (d) making prescription drugs available to others for whom they were not prescribed; (e) keeping other substances knowing that others were abusing them; (f) residing with others who are illegally abusing substances; (g) accompanying others while they illegally abuse substances. For each activity you identified, promptly modify your behavior so as no longer to engage in it. Consult your lawyer about any other activity that you suspect may implicate similar liability and other legal concerns. **Score [___]**

Available law services: drunk-driving defense; driver's license restoration; defense of dram-shop claims; defense of social-host liability claims; defense of drug-possession and drug-dealing or delivery charges; obtaining personal-protection and restraining orders against illegal drug activity.

Your Violations

Criminal statutes and civil liability are not the only laws affecting your conduct. We now live in Regulation Nation. Legislatures at all levels have given federal, state, and local administrative agencies more power than ever to promulgate and enforce regulations. Regulations cover consumer subjects so diverse as food, drugs, cosmetics, toys, guns, fireworks, playground equipment, ladders, tools, batteries, every other consumer product, warnings, daycare, foster care, adoption, housing, camping, campfires, motor vehicles, motorcycles, fuels, boating, liveries, livestock, pets, fundraising, gambling, mowing lawns, burning leaves, other yard-waste disposal, recycling, home-schooling, and hundreds of other goods, services, and activities, many of which you cannot imagine. Regulations are so extensive and grow so quickly that you have little hope of knowing what things that you own, control, or do are subject to them. In such a regulatory environment, the responsible thing to do is to respect regulatory authority.

Know that regulators can issue citations for regulatory violations that could result in heavy fines, orders to cease and desist, and even imprisonment in the worst of cases. Regulators in most situations are interested only in stopping and correcting regulatory violations. The moment that you receive any kind of notice or information that you may be involved in regulatory violations, stop the suspicious activity. If you need or want to continue that activity, then get your lawyer's regulatory review.

Audit: Identify in which of the following potentially suspicious activities subject to regulatory investigation you may be involved: (a) storing more fuel than your lawnmower requires; (b) selling or re-selling fireworks to others; (c) making anything that resembles a gun; (d) growing anything to smoke or ingest for pain or recreation; (e) preparing any food for sale other than at a bake sale; (f) using any chemical on your lawn or garden not commercially manufactured and sold for that purpose; (g) modifying your home at an expense greater than $500 without official review and approval; (h) installing a wood-burning stove; (i) burning grass or leaves; (j) bringing goats, pigs, chickens, or other livestock into a suburban or urban area; (k) holding an outdoor event for public admission; (l) showing a film to anyone other than a few family members and friends; (m) conducting a fundraiser with a raffle or gambling; (n) bringing anyone other than a family member into your home to live in exchange for rent. Research administrative regulations for any of these or similar activities in which you engage, or consult with your lawyer. **Score [___]**

Available Law Services: researching administrative regulations for present or planned activity; reviewing administrative request for investigation; preparing for administrative inspection; producing evidence in response to administrative request; defense of administrative citation.

3 Your Education

Get educated! Actually, the fact that you are reading this page indicates how earnest you are about improving your situation through learning and education. Law has a lot to say about education because education is so critically important to our welfare and the welfare of our families, communities, and nation. While policymakers promote education through curriculum, staffing, and funding measures, they also do so through law, rule, and regulation. This part of your legal audit helps you determine whether you are making the most of your educational rights, responsibilities, and opportunities. Law can help you even when it comes to your education and the education of your family members.

Your Access

You and your family members have certain federal and state protections ensuring your access to public education. State constitutions and laws guarantee basic rights to public grade-school education. Those laws require schools to enroll children within their districts and may require schools to consider requests for out-of-district enrollments. Federal and state laws also require school officials to enroll homeless children. State truancy laws require children to attend school. State laws may require school officials to investigate why certain students are not attending before suspending them for absences. Federal and state labor laws prohibit certain child labor, particularly as that labor would interfere with childhood education. Successive federal acts continue to establish federal educational guidelines relating to federal funding standards. The federal Individuals with Disabilities Education Act (IDEA) requires that grade schools provide disabled children free appropriate education in the least restrictive environment, auguring greater integration of disabled students into general programs, a right that extends to both academic and extra-curricular programs. Federal and state civil rights act guarantee equal access to education, prohibiting discrimination based on sex and race, and other forms of discrimination and retaliation. The U.S. and state constitutions protect freedom of religion, free speech, and freedom of association from public-school interference. In short, you have substantial legal protection for pursuing your education and the education of your family. Use those protections as necessary to take full advantage of your educational rights and interests. Do not let barriers keep you from education. Get your lawyer's help where you encounter obstacles.

Audit: Identify which of the following circumstances may be interfering with your education or the education of your family members: (a) school-district residency or other enrollment disputes; (b) exclusion from classrooms or programs over allegedly disruptive behavior; (c) exclusion from programs based on race, sex, or other personal characteristics; (d) disputes over attendance and excused or unexcused absences; (e) approvals for tutors, aides, counselors, or other professional help with academics or behavior; (f) disagreements with the school over medication or other therapeutic regimens; (g) discipline, suspension, dismissal, or other retaliation for religious views, symbols, or clothing; (h) discipline, suspension, dismissal, or other retaliation for political or artistic expression; (i) disagreements over transportation to and from school. Consult a lawyer knowledgeable in school law for each issue that you identified or for any similar access issue. **Score [___]**

Available Law Services: representing you and your child in disputes over enrollment within a school district; representing you and your disabled child in meetings, hearings, and lawsuits regarding developing or modifying individualized education plans; representing you and your child in suspension or dismissal hearings; representing you and your child in truancy petitions and hearings; representing you and your child as to discrimination claims.

Your Safety

School shootings and other increasing incidents of violence and bullying have rocked public confidence in school safety. Federal and state laws prohibit guns in schools, while state laws often expand that protection to bar other weapons. Schools regularly expel students who bring a weapon to school under rules that may also provide for the expelled student's interim education and later reinstatement. Many state laws also prohibit or limit teachers' use of force, or corporal punishment, to discipline students. Federal and state laws also prohibit harassment particularly when based on a student's race, sex, disability, or other protected characteristic. Some states have also adopted anti-bullying measures. A federal law known as the Clery Act requires colleges and universities to warn about ongoing crimes presenting a serious threat and to disclose information in public logs on crimes that occur on and adjacent to campus. The Clery Act also requires disclosure of sexual assaults, protects sexual-assault victims, and requires registered sex-offender and emergency-response-system notices. You have substantial legal rights and protections relating to school safety. You and your family members should feel and be safe when attending school to enjoy the full benefit of education. Get your lawyer's help if you or your family members face safety threats.

Audit: Identify which of the following conditions may be threatening your safety or the safety of your family members when attending school: (a) evidence or suspicions of weapons at school; (b) student fights or other physical intimidation; (c) evidence of students bullying other students; (d) evidence of students sexually harassing other students; (e) teachers spanking, paddling, or using other forms corporal punishment; (f) suspicions of teachers inappropriately hugging or touching students as intimate behavior; (g) suspicions of teachers having sexual affairs with or dating students; (h) distribution or use of illegal drugs among students at school; (i) viewing or distribution of pornography or sexting at school. Consult a lawyer knowledgeable in school law for each issue that you identified or for any similar safety issue. **Score [___]**

Available Law Services: representing you when reporting unsafe conditions at school; obtaining Clery Act information for your review; protecting you against school retaliation for safety reports or information requests; representing you in making claims against a school or schoolteachers and officials for assault, battery, harassment, and retaliation; representing you when reporting school crimes to law-enforcement officials.

Your Hearing

Schools must maintain an orderly academic environment if students are to learn. They may adopt and enforce reasonable policies to ensure the safety and integrity of school operations. School officials sometimes err in applying those policies. For instance, you or your child may suffer a school suspension or dismissal over false allegations of wrongdoing. The U.S. Constitution and state constitutions require that government provide notice of the alleged wrongdoing and give you an opportunity to respond at a hearing before government denies you or your child a property or liberty interest. While a school may suspend a student immediately without hearing for emergency safety reasons, public schools must then provide the suspended student with notice and opportunity for hearing before continuing to deny the student educational rights. If you or your child face continued suspension or dismissal because of false allegations of wrongdoing, then get the help of a lawyer knowledgeable in school law to preserve and restore your educational rights after hearing. Hearings may be before school officials, the school board, or a local or federal court. For example, school officials in some states must file a truancy petition with the local juvenile court before expelling or otherwise taking long-term action against a student for frequent absences. A juvenile court may order a child's supervision for truancy and may detain a child in juvenile facilities for contempt of truancy orders. Lawyers know hearing procedures and the substantive standards that hearing officials will apply. Get your lawyer's help for educational hearings.

Audit: Identify with which of the following skills you would need your lawyer's help in a school hearing: (a) demanding the school's notice of alleged wrongdoing; (b) demanding a hearing before the appropriate school officials; (c) gathering documentary evidence for use at the hearing; (d) choosing and preparing witnesses for the hearing; (e) making opening statements at the hearing; (f) presenting and authenticating exhibits at the hearing; (g) presenting and questioning witnesses at the hearing; (h) making summaries and arguments at the hearing; (i) citing applicable law, rule, and regulation to hearing decision-makers; (j) supplying written analysis and summaries for decision-makers; (k) reviewing, evaluating, and appealing hearing decisions. **Score [___]**

Available Law Services: representing you at school hearings involving suspension or dismissal; representing you in juvenile court proceedings affecting your child's schooling; representing you or your child in state or federal court due-process claims and hearings.

Your Control

Schools properly design their own environments, establish their own culture, and decide their own curriculum. If traditional schools do not meet your educational goals, then the law provides you with alternatives. Districts in many states must provide alternative high schools for students to complete their diplomas when they cannot or prefer not to do so in their home district. General equivalency diplomas (GEDs) are available online and through alternative classrooms as a substitute for a traditional high school diploma. Law also permits homeschooling as an alternative to compelled grade-school attendance. Under homeschooling laws, parents who choose to keep their children at home for school must notify the school. They must conduct school at home for the required number of hours each day (typically six) and days each year (typically 180). Homeschoolers must provide a curriculum including components similar to those at traditional schools, assess the child at least annually, and maintain records of instruction and assessment. The homeschooling parent must qualify to instruct the child but may usually do so with modest college education. Homeschooling laws typically permit homeschooled children to attend traditional school events and even to choose and attend certain classes. The law gives you substantial control over your education and the education of your children.

Audit: Identify which of the following situations may encourage you to pursue alternative education for yourself or your children: (a) travel; (b) work; (c) arts; (d) athletics; (e) pregnancy; (f) child rearing; (g) personality conflict; (h) cultural conflict; (i) ideology conflict; (j) faith differences; (k) language immersion; (l) creative opportunities; (m) fostering genius.

28

Consult your lawyer if you encounter obstacles to obtaining alternative education. **Score [___]**

Available Law Services: researching rights to alternative education programs; representing you in disputes with school officials over enrollment in alternative programs; researching homeschooling requirements; representing you in disputes with school officials over homeschooling.

Your Savings

Lawmakers know that higher education can be expensive and have taken steps to encourage college saving. Tax laws recognize two college-savings plans known as 529 plans and Coverdell plans. The tax code's Section 529 permits states to operate plans through which you may fund an account for a designated beneficiary such as a child or grandchild to use for college tuition, fees, books, room, and board. While you may not deduct 529-plan contributions from your income for purposes of reducing your income taxes, account earnings and qualifying distributions are tax free. While 529 plans generally do not limit your annual contribution amount, contributions of more than the current $14,000 gift-tax limit may result in your child or other designee owing gift tax. Another type of tax-favored education account is the Education Savings Account (ESA) also known as the Coverdell plan. A Coverdell ESA limits your annual contributions to no more than $2,000. You must designate a qualifying beneficiary, but unlike a Section 529 account, you may designate yourself, not just children or others, as the beneficiary. You may also use a Coverdell ESA to pay expenses not just of higher education but of primary and secondary education. Make the most of your educational opportunities and those of your children by saving for college under tax-law-favored plans. Individuals also leave lasting legacies by providing in wills, trusts, and other estate plans for the private or college education of children, grandchildren, and others. Consider leaving such a legacy.

Audit: Identify those for whom you could or should be saving for college, whether yourself, your children or grandchildren, or others. Estimate the amount you would like to save and the date by which you would like to save it. Then consult your lawyer about how to participate in tax-favored college savings plans. If you already have monies saved that you intend to convey for the education of children, grandchildren, or others, then consult your lawyer about an estate plan that will ensure that those monies go for the purpose you intend. **Score [___]**

Available Law Services: researching and advising you on the terms and qualifications for tax-favored college savings plans; preparing wills, trusts, and other estate plans to provide for the education of others.

Your Loans

You may decide to take out student loans for college or graduate education or to guarantee the student loans of a child, grandchild, or other. Be cautious with student loans. While you may discharge many other types of loan or obligation in the unfortunate event of your bankruptcy, federal bankruptcy laws do not permit discharge of many student loans. Be especially cautious when guaranteeing the loans of others. Chances are good that you, not the borrower, will repay those loans. Lenders seek loan guarantees when they believe that the borrower lacks credit worthiness. Federal laws regulate student-loan programs in other ways that may make them advantageous. The federal government subsidizes some student loans so that loan interest and payments do not begin until a grace period expires following graduation. Law generally requires that lenders permit you to pay student loans off early. Federal law may permit you to defer repayment for unemployment, re-enrollment, graduate fellowship, disability, or financial hardship. Some federal student-loan programs offer partial forgiveness for working in public-interest positions for periods such as ten years. Other laws may offer you graduated repayment plans in which your payments gradually rise over time (presuming that your income will also be rising) or income-sensitive repayment tying payments to the level of your income.

Audit: List and total the current balances and current or anticipated monthly payment on all of your student loans, if you have any. Are you able to pay or (if you have not yet begun paying) will you be able to pay for those loans? If not, then consult your lawyer regarding your deferment, graduated-repayment, income-sensitive-repayment, and loan-forgiveness options. If you cannot answer that question, then develop a budget making your best estimate of your monthly income and expenses. If that budget indicates that you will be unable to pay, then consult your lawyer as above. **Score [___]**

Available Law Services: reviewing and evaluating loan-guarantee requests; researching and advising you on loan-deferment, graduated-repayment, income-sensitive-repayment, and loan-forgiveness options; helping you document and complete loan-deferment requests; representing you in appeals of loan-deferment denials; defending you in loan-repayment and loan-guarantee actions.

4 Your Housing

The law has a lot to say about your housing. Everyone needs a place to live. Shelter is such a basic need that in law it approaches a civil right. Even the homeless or others in need of emergency shelter have certain protections of the law, with which the first section below deals. The law also provides substantial protection to renters, which the second section below describes. The law also regulates home purchases and sales, and the rights, obligations, and advantages of home owners, including in the mortgages that they use to secure financing of home purchases. Home insurance raises and addresses other law issues. A home is the largest asset that most of us purchase in a lifetime. The laws addressing its purchase or sale, financing, security, and protection mean a lot to us. Consider below these and other rights, responsibilities, and opportunities that you have regarding your housing.

Your Shelter

We all hope to have secure shelter at all times. Yet none of us are immune from the natural and human-caused disasters, domestic violence, and other events that can leave any of us in need of emergency shelter. The law provides the homeless with

33

certain protections. We all get to use public spaces with reasonable security for our persons and effects, even when we have no private residence and must instead rely on those public spaces for shelter. Courts have granted constitutional protection against law-enforcement actions involving unreasonable search, seizure, and disposition of personal effects, and against arrests for loitering. State and local laws create homeless-assistance programs, some laws requiring law-enforcement officers to offer emergency shelter before taking other actions to arrest or remove homeless persons and dispose of their personal effects. Federal law authorizes special programs for the housing, care, and education of runaway and homeless youth. Federal and state laws authorize subsidies to transition individuals and families from emergency shelter into apartments with rent tied to household income. Once in housing, you have further legal support to defend yourself and family members there against violence and threats of violence. State laws authorize restraining orders to remove violent family members or other individuals from your home and personal-protection orders to keep them from threatening your security in and around your housing. Public-interest lawyers, legal-aid lawyers, and family lawyers may deal frequently with emergency-shelter issues. Consult your lawyer if you or someone about whom you care needs the law's help with housing.

Audit: Which of the following issues does your community face with respect to emergency shelter? (a) Inadequate 2-1-1 or other social-assistance referral system. (b) Insufficient number of emergency-shelter beds. (c) Loitering and panhandling reducing personal security and interfering with tourism or business. (d) Law-enforcement mistreatment of the homeless. (e) Inadequate access to the courts for restraining and personal-protection orders. (f) Insufficient quantity of transitional, subsidized housing. (g) Landlord discrimination against homeless prospective tenants. (h) Inadequate law enforcement for victims of domestic violence. (i)

Inadequate legal relief for victims of natural or human-caused disasters. **Score [___]**

Available Law Services: representing you to obtain a restraining order or personal-protection order to ensure your continued housing; representing you to challenge an unnecessary restraint obtained by others affecting your housing; providing referrals to emergency shelter; researching and advocating your transitional, subsidized-housing options; investigating suspected housing discrimination against you; evaluating your police-misconduct claims affecting your personal security and effects; defending you against loitering or similar charges.

Your Renting

The law gives you substantial support when you have issues or concerns around renting your housing. State laws closely regulate the relationship between landlords and tenants. Those laws prohibit or limit landlord practices that would put tenants at disadvantages around issues like charging, holding, and returning security deposits, serving timely eviction notices, and charging for cleaning the apartment after tenancy terminates. Other laws impose duties on landlords to maintain apartments in safe conditions with smoke alarms and deadbolt door locks, and habitable conditions with working plumbing, heating, and electricity. State laws also require landlords to ensure tenants' quiet enjoyment of the premises, meaning that landlords may have to abate noise, odors, pests, drug dealing, prostitution, and other disruptive conditions and activities. State law may permit you to withhold or escrow that part of your rent representing the lost value of uninhabitable parts of your apartment or lost enjoyment. State and federal laws prohibit race, sex, and religious discrimination in renting, while laws also prohibit landlords from banning families with children. Outside of these statutory protections, the lease itself will determine your rights and obligations including the amount of your rent, the duration of your tenancy, whether you may keep pets, and what access you may have to common areas and amenities like pools, exercise rooms, and tennis or basketball courts. Read your lease before signing. Consult your lawyer whenever you suspect violation of your rights as a tenant or have a dispute with your landlord over the terms and conditions of your tenancy.

Audit: If you are renting, then confirm that you know the following terms and preferably that you have them in writing: (a) monthly rent amount; (b) lease term, meaning when it ends; (c) whether you have the option to renew the lease at its expiration; (d) whether rent increases with renewal; (e) security deposit you paid; (f) description of any damage to your unit when rented to you; (g) rights you have to use amenities like laundry service and recreational facilities; (h) rights you have to pets. If you have issues, disputes, or concerns over these or other terms, then consult your lawyer. **Score [___]**

Available Law Services: negotiating lease terms on your behalf; advising you on your tenant rights; preparing notices, requests, and demands regarding your lease rights; exercising renewal options for you; representing you in lawsuits between you and your landlord over lease and habitation rights; investigating your claims for housing discrimination and representing you in those claims.

Your Buying

Buying your home is one of the biggest financial decisions you will ever make. Law has a lot to say about the terms and conditions of your home purchase both to protect you as the buyer and to protect the seller. When a seller advertises a home, the seller must not misrepresent conditions of the home. A buyer who reasonably relies on a seller's knowing misrepresentations, particularly as to hidden conditions that the buyer cannot readily discover, may recover the attendant loss. Some states require sellers to complete a disclosure statement describing conditions of the home. Otherwise, the general rule is for the buyer to beware, meaning that the buyer should include a home-inspection contingency in the sale contract. Buyers also often include a financing contingency in the sale contract to ensure that their mortgage commitment will apply to the purchase of the home. Buyer and seller sign a purchase contract that includes these and other important terms including the form of the deed, the seller's title-insurance obligation, pre-close walk-through inspection, and closing date. Contracts often include a contingency for attorney review to ensure that the contract contains appropriate clauses. If contractor inspection or walk-through inspection reveal material defects, then negotiations over price reductions may ensue. With the help of legal counsel, buyers must also inspect closely the title-insurance commitment for exclusions to be sure that the property is free from encumbrances. Federal and state laws protect prospective buyers from sellers unwilling to sell because of race, sex, religious, or similar discrimination.

Audit: If you are buying a home, then ensure that you understand and are able to negotiate the following terms in your purchase contract: (a) fair price; (b) reasonable refundable earnest money; (c) financing contingency; (d) contractor-inspection contingency; (e) attorney-review contingency; (f) seller's disclosure statement; (g) seller's title insurance for clear title; (h) warranty deed; (i) reasonable closing date; (j) possession at closing; (k) tax pro-ration to closing; (l) pre-close walk-through inspection; (m) seller pays transfer taxes. If you do not understand or cannot negotiate these terms, then consult and retain your lawyer to do so. **Score [___]**

Available Law Services: negotiating sale price and terms; drafting or reviewing purchase agreement; obtaining and reviewing seller's disclosure statement; reviewing and evaluating inspection results; negotiating price reductions over needed repairs; reviewing title-insurance commitment and exceptions;

conducting or attending purchase closing; representing you in seller-fraud claims; investigating fair-housing claims and representing you in making those claims.

Your Mortgage

The law also says a lot about how you finance your home. Few of us buy a home, especially a first home, without borrowing money to pay for it. Banks lend money for home purchases only by taking a mortgage as security for your repayment of the loan. Federal and state laws govern mortgages. For example, when you apply for a mortgage, your written application represents your creditworthiness. You must represent your income, assets, and debts accurately, or you may have committed federal or state crimes. Similarly, the bank must represent to you the terms of your loan accurately, particularly as to floating interest rates, balloon payments, late fees, and other terms that may harm or disadvantage borrowers later. Banks that fail to disclose material terms or otherwise deal unfairly with already-disadvantaged borrowers may violate laws and rules against predatory lending. Conversely, banks that refuse to lend to the already-disadvantaged may face regulatory sanctions and liability for a racially discriminatory practice known as *redlining*. Beyond these and other federal and state statutory and regulatory controls, the law of mortgages has primarily to do with its contract terms. A mortgage is an agreement that the lender take control of the property in the event of the borrower's default. Just as important as the mortgage's foreclosure terms (with which the next section deals) are the terms of the accompanying note including the interest rate, whether the rate is fixed or floats, the period over which you must repay the loan, the resulting monthly payment, whether you must carry mortgage insurance, and other monetary terms. Both borrower and lender must approach mortgage transactions with caution to comply with the law, which only makes sense given the individual and national significance of mortgage transactions.

Audit: If you are a homeowner with a mortgage, then identify the following terms and conditions: (a) what bank or entity currently holds and administers your mortgage; (b) the current interest rate on your mortgage; (c) the current interest rate on new mortgages; (d) your mortgage balance; (e) whether your mortgage payments are current; (f) the mortgage term (date of final payment); (g) whether you are paying for mortgage insurance; (h) whether you now qualify to drop mortgage insurance or can purchase it for less through term life insurance. If you are unable to confirm this information, have questions over what it means, or believe that you may be able to gain better terms in a refinance, then consult your lawyer. **Score [＿]**

Available Law Services: reviewing and correcting credit history; reviewing and completing mortgage applications; evaluating mortgage and note options and offers; investigating discriminatory denials of mortgage applications, and representing you in discrimination claims; reviewing mortgage and note documentation; reviewing and evaluating mortgage-handling practices for law violations; reviewing and challenging late charges, fees, and other charges affecting mortgage balances; representing you in disputes over mortgage balances and negotiating settlements of those disputes.

Your Foreclosure

Mortgages give lenders the right to foreclose on your home in the event of your default. To foreclose means to take control of the home, begin a process to remove you from the home, and eventually sell the home to pay as much of the remaining mortgage balance as possible. Federal and state laws closely regulate mortgage foreclosures. Some states require lenders to foreclose only through a court proceeding, while other states permit lenders to foreclose without going to court. In either case, the lender must give you proper notice of your default, giving you a chance to dispute default, bring your balance current, or seek replacement financing to keep your home. If you do not wish to keep the home, then you may be able to provide the bank with your deed to the home instead of going through foreclosure. Foreclosure affects your future ability to obtain credit. The outcome of foreclosure typically depends on whether the home is worth more than the mortgage balance. Homeowners whose homes are worth less than their mortgage balance may face a deficiency balance and personal liability even after the home's foreclosure and sale. Federal, state, and lender programs address and discourage mortgage foreclosures. You may qualify for deferred payments, reductions in payments, or reductions in your mortgage balance under those programs. Act promptly to consult your lawyer in the event that you fall behind or expect to fall behind in payments.

Audit: If you have fallen behind on your mortgage payment or expect to do so, then take these steps: (a) develop a written budget; (b) adjust your budget to attempt to remain current on your mortgage; (c) notify the lender in writing, requesting information on the lender's mortgage-relief programs for which you qualify; (d) research federal and state mortgage-relief programs for which you qualify; (e) determine the value of your home, comparing it to your mortgage balance; (f) determine whether you wish to keep the home; (g) confirm your plan of action for the best possible outcome. Then consult your lawyer regarding what you learned and planned. **Score [___]**

Available Law Services: reviewing mortgage and note documentation for assignments between lenders; reviewing and evaluating mortgage-handling practices for law violations; reviewing and challenging late charges, fees, and other charges affecting mortgage balances; representing you in disputes over mortgage balances and negotiating settlements of those disputes; defending you in foreclosure actions; helping you identify mortgage-relief programs for which you qualify and helping you apply to those programs; preparing your deed to the lender in lieu of foreclosure and otherwise helping you protect your credit.

Your Insurance

Your home is a significant financial asset that you should be protecting with homeowner's insurance. Homeowner's insurance typically protects you against loss of or damage to the home due to fire, lightning, high wind, hail, or other natural or artificial accident or occurrence. Homeowner's coverage begins with the cost of the home's repair or replacement. Homeowner's coverage also typically includes repair or replacement of the home's contents, meaning your personal effects inside and around the home. Proving everything that you owned after a fire destroyed it can be a significant challenge. Consider video-recording everything you own in a quick annual tour of your home. Your homeowner's coverage may also pay for temporary housing in an apartment or hotel during your home's repair. State laws regulate the insurance industry closely to ensure the protection for which you bargained. Some of those laws have to do with requiring insurance companies to maintain adequate reserves so that they are financially able to pay you when you suffer insured losses. Other provisions may protect you against unfair or hidden policy terms and exclusions. When you apply for a homeowner's policy, be sure to make accurate and complete disclosures. False material disclosures, particularly those affecting the insurer's risk, may void the policy. Notify the insurer promptly in writing if you intend to operate a business in your home, install a wood-burning stove, store chemicals, or conduct any other activity that increases the insurer's risk or that the insurance application asked you to disclose. Consult your lawyer in the event of any question over insurance coverage, whenever preparing proof of significant loss, or about any dispute with your insurer.

Audit: If you own a home, then obtain your homeowner's insurance policy and its declarations page or cover sheet to confirm each of the following: (a) that the value for which the policy insures your home at least equals its current appraised value; (b) that the policy's contents coverage approximates the value of your contents, usually equal to or greater than the home's value; (c) that the policy does not exclude any specific contents such as valuable collectibles or artwork that you have in the home; (d) that the policy does not exclude any condition such as fireplace, wood-burning stove, sauna, or spa that you currently have in the home; (e) that you are not conducting any excluded business use in the home. Also, obtain a copy of your insurance application to confirm its accuracy and correct any omission. Consult your lawyer over any issues this review raises. **Score [___]**

Available Law Services: confirming and explaining your coverage, limits, and exclusions; preparing and documenting claim of loss; investigating and proving cause of loss; preparing and defending you in examinations under oath; representing you in actions against your insurer for coverage; obtaining and proving loss appraisals; negotiating coverage settlements.

Your Enjoyment

The law grants you certain rights and opportunities as the owner of your home. Single-family homeowners usually own in fee-simple title, meaning the strongest bundle of rights to use, control, alter, and improve the premises while excluding others, and to convey the premises gaining any appreciation in its sale. Condominium owners share limited interests in the whole while having exclusive access to their part, without the unilateral right to alter or improve. Your right to exclude others from your home means that you may pursue civil action or criminal charge for trespass against those who enter whether or not they cause any damage. State nuisance laws give you a right of civil action to stop others from interfering with your use and enjoyment of your home because of noise, odor, light, smoke, and similar offenses. Others may have easement rights particularly to maintain utilities but also possibly to cross your property to access other properties. Easements may arise by continuous adverse use such as when others cross your property for an extended period along a defined path. You may even lose ownership to parts of your property if a neighbor or another builds a structure, driveway, or fence on your property and maintains it there for an extended time. Zoning laws and building codes may restrict your ability to improve your property in the manner that you desire. Consult your lawyer whenever you have any disputes over your ownership, control, use, enjoyment, or improvement of your home.

Audit: If you own a home, then confirm your satisfaction with each of the following rights: (a) your clear title to the home; (b) your ability to exclude others from entering your property; (c) your enjoyment of your home free from interference; (d) your ability to maintain your premises as you wish to; (e) your ability to improve your home as you desire. Consult your lawyer if you are dissatisfied with any of the above or with similar rights and privileges of home ownership. **Score [___]**

Available Law Services: settling title to your home including removing any clouds on or claims to your title; representing you in disputes with your condominium association over use or improvement; demanding that others cease trespassing on your land, and obtaining orders preventing trespass; representing you in civil actions to recover for damage to or theft from your home or land; representing you in disputes with neighbors over boundaries, fences, decks, driveways, and other improvements or structures encroaching on your land; representing you in disputes with zoning or building officials over your maintenance or improvement of your home; advocating for zoning variances for out-of-code improvements.

43

Your Obligations

Along with your rights and privileges of home ownership, the law imposes certain obligations around owning a home. One obligation has to do with paying property taxes. Property taxes can be substantial even to the point of forcing low-income long-time homeowners out of their home. Failure to pay property taxes may result in the tax sale of your home after appropriate notice. Jurisdictions assess property taxes based on the value of your home. Because values are uncertain, state laws provide you with procedures to challenge the public appraiser's valuation. Read the annual appraisal notice that you receive from the tax assessor. Satisfy yourself that the annual change in value is in line with changes in the real estate market and that your home assessment is fair. Invoke the challenge and appeal procedures when the assessment is unfair. Another obligation that state laws impose is that you not conduct activities on your property that interfere with the health, safety, and welfare of the public or that interfere with the rights of adjacent property owners to enjoy their own property. Avoid bright lights shining into neighboring residences late at night, loud music or parties, smoke from bonfires, odors from garbage or refuse, fights and loitering around basketball courts, and similar disturbances. Local ordinances may also require that you keep lawns reasonably mown, clean up brush and leaves, and otherwise maintain the grounds around your home. Local ordinance may require you to pay for repair of the public sidewalk in front of your home and to pay assessments for repair or improvement of walks, streets, and utilities serving your home. You must also comply with zoning restrictions not to conduct unauthorized commercial, industrial, agricultural, or other activities in your home.

Audit: If own your home, then determine the value for which the tax assessor has appraised it, and compare that value to its market value. If its assessed value exceeds its market value, then consult your lawyer about challenging the assessment at the next annual opportunity. **Score [___]**

Available Law Services: representing you in challenges and appeals of tax appraisals; challenging tax sale of your home; defending you in nuisance actions brought by neighbors or members of the public; representing you in disputes with your local government over your maintenance of the grounds around your home; challenging local-government assessments for repair and improvement of public facilities serving your home; advocating for improvements and assessments in your interest; representing you in zoning disputes over activities you conduct in and around your home.

Your Selling

The law also regulates closely your sale of your home. When you list your home for sale with a real estate agent, the agent owes you the duties under the listing agreement, just as you owe the agent the duties and percentage fee under the same agreement. Read and consider the listing agreement carefully. To prospective buyers, you owe the legal duty not to misrepresent your home's condition. Do not distort, disguise, exaggerate, or minimize the actual condition of your home, whether orally or in brochures or other advertising. State law may also require that you complete a seller's disclosure statement. Read the statement carefully, and answer each required disclosure completely and truthfully. Misrepresentations or omissions from the disclosure statement may lead to your civil liability to the buyer. When you enter into a sale agreement with a buyer, read the agreement carefully to ensure that you agree and can comply with the price, earnest-money, financing and inspection contingencies, closing date, and all other terms. Expect to pro-rate the property taxes to the closing date. Negotiate who pays any federal, state, or local transfer tax. Expect to provide and pay for title insurance. Homes often appreciate in value, giving you the opportunity to benefit financially from your home's sale. Be sure that the sale price will satisfy all mortgages, commissions, taxes, and other costs of sale.

Be sure that you have the full right to sell and do not share that right with separated or former spouses, relatives, land-contract holders, or others who must approve your sale and may claim an interest in your sale proceeds.

Audit: Which of the following home-sale steps do you feel qualified to complete? (a) Negotiating and entering into a fair listing agreement. (b) Completing an accurate and complete seller's disclosure statement. (c) Negotiating a fair sale price. (d) Approving a fair sale agreement. (e) Responding to demands for price reductions after inspections. (f) Obtaining and correcting title-insurance commitment. (g) Calculating tax pro-ration to closing date. (h) Preparing or reviewing the sale deed. (i) Conducting the closing. Consult and retain your lawyer for any of the above sale tasks for which you are not qualified. **Score [___]**

Available Law Services: reviewing and negotiating a listing agreement; helping you prepare a seller's disclosure statement; negotiating a sale price; providing, completing, reviewing, and revising a sale agreement; conducting the closing or representing you at the closing of the sale; reviewing and addressing terms of the title-insurance commitment; representing you in disputes with buyers.

5 Your Transportation

Safe and efficient transportation is critical to your success and well-being, so much so that you know the law will have a lot to say about it. Law heavily regulates public transportation by taxicab, limousine, bus, train, boat, and plane but also private motor vehicles in particular, not only their design, manufacture, sale, and operation, but also their titling, recall, repair, and insurance. The law in each of these areas can provide you with substantial rights and protections while simultaneously imposing specific liabilities and obligations. Consider the following sections on your purchase, titling, insurance, operation, and accidents with your own motor vehicle. Consult your lawyer when you have law concerns, questions, or issues relating to your transportation.

Your Purchase

Law closely regulates certain conditions relating to your purchase of a vehicle. Truth-in-lending laws require dealers to disclose financing terms including finance charges, loan duration, monthly payments, and annual interest rate. Co-signers also get a notice. Vehicle sellers often make more profit on the vehicle's financing than on the vehicle sale price, making financing a situation of buyer beware. Financing the vehicle means that you must maintain your payments or may lose the vehicle to repossession. While you should receive notice of your default in payments and generally will receive demands for payment, do not expect notice that the finance company is about to repossess your vehicle. Commercial codes permit repossession of the vehicle from the public street, your driveway, your workplace, or any other location where repossession does not breach the peace. Once repossessed, your vehicle may sell at wholesale auction for a price less than the amount you owe, leaving you responsible to pay the deficiency. If the finance company pursues a civil judgment against you for that deficiency, then it may garnish your wages or bank accounts. Vehicle leasing can be particularly profitable for the dealer and expensive for you when you consider the up-front payment, annual mileage limit, and lease buy-out terms. Consumer-leasing laws thus require disclosure of those and other terms. Vehicle manufacturers must also disclose fuel mileage. While sellers of new vehicles will owe vehicle warranties, used-vehicle sellers may generally disclaim warranties, meaning that you buy the vehicle as it is. Check a used vehicle's accident and repair history, and have a qualified mechanic inspect it before purchase. Consult your lawyer if you have issues or disputes over your purchase or financing of a vehicle.

Audit: Confirm these terms of any vehicle you are currently financing: (a) name and address of the finance company; (b) finance term (last-payment date); (c) monthly payment amount; (d) principal balance owing; (e) annual interest rate; (f) whether you are current on payments; and (g) any recent late or finance charges assessed. If you are leasing a vehicle, then confirm these terms: (a) name and address of the lease company; (b) lease duration (last-payment date); (c) lease buy out amount; (d) annual mileage limit; (e) per-mile charge for miles over limit; (f) whether you are current on payments; and (g) any recent late or finance charges assessed. Consult your lawyer if you have any disagreement or dispute over these terms. **Score [___]**

Available Law Services: reviewing and advising you on financing terms; reviewing and advising you regarding lease terms; investigating and representing you in misrepresentation claims regarding vehicle purchase; negotiating settlements with vehicle finance companies over allegedly delinquent accounts; defending you in civil actions to recover deficiency judgment after vehicle repossession and sale; negotiating or obtaining an installment judgment to forestall or prevent wage or account garnishment.

Your Title

Vehicles are so mobile and easily stolen, converted, or otherwise transferred that state laws create vehicle-title systems to preserve some order and control for vehicle owners, financers, buyers, and sellers. A title is a document proving your ownership that you should keep in a secure place with your other legal and financial papers. When you bought your vehicle, the seller gave you a title indicating your ownership. States issue new titles to new owners of vehicles. A seller completes transfer of title by signing the title over to the buyer who applies for the new title in the buyer's own name. If you financed your vehicle, then the finance company will have placed a lien on your vehicle title preventing you from selling the vehicle with title unless you pay off the financing and get the finance-company release. Registration is different from title. While state laws create vehicle-title systems, they separately require annual registration of vehicles operated on the public highways. When you register your new vehicle or renew your registration each year, you get documentary proof of current registration that you must keep in the vehicle to show to law-enforcement officials. You also get a new license plate or tag to display on the vehicle confirming the lawfulness of its operation on the public highways. Consider carefully how you title and register your vehicle. States have owner-consent laws under which all those who hold title to a vehicle or register the vehicle owe personal liability to anyone whom a consensual user of the vehicle injures negligently. Consult your lawyer about how to title and register your vehicle to ensure your ownership and control while reducing your liability.

Audit: Confirm each person who is on each vehicle title and registration for vehicles operated by members of your household. Consult your lawyer about the best way to title and register vehicles to maintain ownership and control but reduce the risk of personal liability for injuries caused by consensual users. **Score [___]**

Available Law Services: helping you obtain replacement title for lost or stolen title; helping you transfer title; helping you obtain release of lien on title; advising you on titling and registering your vehicles to reduce liability risk; defending you against actions for owner-consent liability; notifying your liability insurers to invoke coverage and defense for owner-consent liability.

Your Insurance

State laws require motor-vehicle owners to maintain insurance on vehicles operated on the public highways. Your failure to maintain the required vehicle insurance may result in civil liability and infractions or criminal charges, and loss of important rights and immunities. States have different systems for enforcing vehicle-insurance laws, with which vast numbers of vehicle owners fail to comply. Beyond the above penalties including conviction, fine, and incarceration, some states will boot-lock or confiscate vehicles. Maintain insurance on any vehicle you own and operate on the public highways. The risks of not doing so are significant and serious. Insurance laws dictate the terms and conditions for motor-vehicle insurance. Those laws differ widely from state to state. Some states mandate no-fault systems that grant generous insurance benefits without respect to fault while barring most fault-based rights of action. Other states follow traditional fault-based systems in which negligent drivers and the owners of negligently driven vehicles owe liability to those injured or whose vehicles or property suffer damage. In both systems, whether you choose to insure your vehicle for collision loss is a significant consideration. In both systems, the policy limits that you choose and pay for, and whether you purchase uninsured-motorist or underinsured-motorist coverage, are other significant considerations. Consult your lawyer about your insurance obligations, rights, and coverage, to ensure that you have the right protection.

Audit: Obtain from your files or insurance agent a copy of your motor-vehicle insurance policy, declarations page, and all riders and addenda. Then determine the following: (a) identity of all named insured operators; (b) identity of all other persons covered as an insured under policy definitions; (c) identity of any excluded drivers who must not operate your vehicle (for whom the insurer will provide no coverage); (d) identity of all vehicles insured; (d) liability limits; (e) whether you have uninsured-motorist coverage, and if so, the applicable limits; (f) whether you have underinsured-motorist coverage, and if so, the applicable limits. Consult your lawyer if you have any question or concern about what these terms mean to your rights and obligations. Consult your lawyer for a review of each of these terms. **Score [___]**

Available Law Services: reviewing your insurance coverage and advising you as to gaps or duplication; representing you in disputes with your insurer over coverage or benefits; defending you in liability claims and invoking liability coverage and defense from your insurer.

Your Maintenance

Law also regulates certain rights and obligations relating to your maintenance of your vehicle. For example, state and federal law regulate vehicle warranties. State commercial codes impose the requirement that new vehicles and other consumer goods be merchantable, meaning that they be fit for their ordinary purpose as you would expect them to perform. Vehicle manufacturers offer specific new-vehicle express warranties beyond the implied merchantability warranty. Read your warranty for the express terms, which typically provide for powertrain and other basic repair for three to four years or 36,000 to 48,000 miles. Federal law prohibits dealers from voiding vehicle warranties if you have others perform routine maintenance. You do not have to have the dealer do routine maintenance to preserve your warranty. Some states require used-vehicle dealers to warrant basic repairs for vehicle use or safety for limited miles or periods depending on the vehicle mileage. Some states also require used-vehicle dealers and private-party used-vehicle sellers to disclose defects. States have also enacted lemon laws for new vehicles but in some states also for used vehicles. Lemon laws require dealers to repurchase vehicles if the dealer cannot repair a persistent defect. Otherwise, used-vehicle dealers are free to sell used vehicles as is, with all faults, meaning without warranty. When you have a mechanic repair your vehicle, state laws permit mechanics to retain the vehicle as security for your payment, known as a mechanic's lien. Vehicle-towing and storage companies may claim similar liens. State laws also regulate repair estimates and return of repaired parts. Manufacturers may issue recalls of your vehicle, meaning to offer free repair of manufacturing and design defects. Manufacturers and dealers sometimes benefit from recalls in terms of new-vehicle sales, so much so that new laws are regulating recall notices. Consult your lawyer if you face issues over your vehicle's warranty, maintenance, and repair.

Audit: Identify any express or implied warranty you have remaining for any vehicle in your household. Do vehicles in your household require replacement or repair that may be under those warranties? Consult your lawyer regarding your warranty rights and claims. **Score [___]**

Available Law Services: reviewing and evaluating your warranty claims; representing you in advocating for warranty coverage; invoking lemon law for repurchase of your vehicle; representing you in disputes over repair and mechanic's liens.

Your Operation

State traffic safety codes closely regulate your operation of motor vehicles. Every driver knows the basic rules of the road. Many drivers deliberately break those rules. You must have a valid driver's license to use the public highways. Yet many individuals operate vehicles without a driver's license or with a revoked or suspended license. Penalties for doing so can be severe. Indeed, penalties for many traffic-safety violations increase when accidents are involved. Speeding or other reckless driving will get you a ticket. Speeding or other reckless driving causing accidental injury or death can result in a heavy fine, community service, and even jail or prison sentence. Accidents are unpredictable. You never know when conditions will suddenly arise to cause an unavoidable accident or when your attention will lapse to cause an avoidable accident. Comply with traffic-safety laws at all times. Be certain to comply with child-restraint laws and other safety provisions, particularly those having to do with drunk driving, when transporting children. Violating those laws could not only result in serious injury to a child but to abuse and neglect proceedings and restriction or termination of parental rights. When you receive a charge or citation for allegedly operating a vehicle unlawfully, you have rights to due process, meaning that you may request a hearing before a judge or magistrate to contest the charge or citation. Infractions can affect your insurance rates, driving privileges, employment, and civil liability. Be sure to treat citations and charges responsibly while cognizant of your legal rights and broader interests.

Audit: How are your driving habits? Do you often deliberately exceed the speed limit? When driving, are you constantly on the lookout to avoid detection by law-enforcement officers? What is your driving record? How many additional infractions could you incur before your driving record adversely affects your driving privileges? Do you pay more for insurance rates because of your poor driving record? Would you remain employed if you lost your driver's license? Consult your lawyer if you have concerns or questions on these issues. **Score [___]**

Available Law Services: researching and advising you on traffic-safety laws; defending you on traffic-safety citations and criminal charges.

Your Accident

The law helps those involved in motor-vehicle accidents defend, protect, assert, and adjust their rights. Vehicle repair or replacement would first depend on whether the vehicle owner purchased collision-loss coverage as part of the motor-vehicle insurance. In such cases, disputes sometimes arise over the insurer's appraisal of the destroyed vehicle's value or over repair costs. Insurance policies may provide for resolving those dispute either through court action or arbitration. When a driver operates a vehicle carelessly, causing injury or loss to another, state common law would ordinarily permit the person suffering injury or loss to recover from the careless driver, who would ordinarily have liability insurance to pay for the defense of the claim and for all or part of the recovery. Under owner-consent laws, vehicle owners would share the liability with the careless driver whom they permitted to use the vehicle. No-fault systems in several states modify these common law liability rules. No-fault systems vary widely in their particulars. In general, though, they offer certain insurance benefits to accident victims without respect to anyone's fault while barring fault claims in all but the most serious cases. Accidents can also result in citations for civil infractions and even criminal charges when an accident results from a driver's violation of the state's traffic safety code. Motor-vehicle accidents cause billions of dollars in losses every year, involving significant, personal, financial, and business interests. Consult your lawyer about your rights and obligations whenever involved in a motor-vehicle accident causing loss or injury.

Audit: If you or a family member for whom you have financial responsibility are involved in a motor-vehicle accident, then consider each of the following: (a) whose fault (assuming any) caused the accident; (b) whether police issued citations; (c) what personal injuries the accident caused, and what medical expense or wage loss resulted; (d) what vehicle loss or damage the accident caused; (e) what real property damage the accident caused; (f) what personal property loss the accident caused; (g) who were the responsible drivers; (h) who owned or registered the involved vehicles; (i) what insurers covered the involved drivers and vehicle owners; (j) what insurers covered the involved vehicles; (k) whether those insurers provided collision coverage. Then consult your lawyer regarding the rights and obligations that attend the accident's circumstances. **Score [___]**

Available Law Services: advising you as to rights and obligations arising out of motor-vehicle accidents in which you or your vehicle or dependent family member were involved; representing you in disputes with your insurer over coverage or benefits following an accident; negotiating a fair recovery based on appraisals for vehicle replacement; reviewing insurance policies to advise you on arbitration and other necessary procedures relating to accident recoveries; representing you in negligence actions against others to recover for your loss, injury, or damage; defending you in liability claims and invoking liability coverage and defense from your insurer; representing you in bad-faith claims against your insurer for refusal to settle.

6 Your Employment

Your employment means a lot to you. The employed draw not only income and benefits like health insurance and retirement plans from their employment but also purpose, respect, relationship, reputation, and meaning. Naturally, then, law has a lot to say about employment, given the substantial interests we each have in employment. Employment law covers the entire spectrum of work from the advertising of jobs through application for jobs, negotiation of terms, hiring, wages, benefits, training, safety, injury, privacy, evaluation, and promotion, right down to medical and family leaves, layoffs, plant closings, unemployment, and termination. Laws protect workers while preserving a sphere, widening in some areas and narrowing in others, within which employers can shape jobs and influence workers to accomplish the tasks that will preserve the enterprise. Consider the following rights and responsibilities while consulting your lawyer whenever you see opportunities in these issues to improve your work and, with it, to improve your life.

Your Recruitment

Your first interest in employment is finding it, with which the law has ways to help you. Law regulates how employers advertise for jobs, and how employees apply for and obtain it, primarily through anti-discrimination laws. Federal and state anti-discrimination laws prohibit employers from advertising and hiring based on race, ethnicity, ancestry, national origin, religion, sex, age, disability, genetics, and, in some states or locales, marital status and orientation. You should not see employers advertising for "young men" or "young women," for instance, except in the very rare cases where a protected category is a bona fide occupational qualification, such as an actor of a certain age, sex, or race to portray a famous person in history of same age, sex, and race, or a religious leader or teacher of a certain faith. Yet federal and state anti-discrimination laws do more than prohibit employers from advertising for racial, sexual, age, and other prohibited preferences. Employers must also avoid using proxies for protected categories, such as "mature" or "attractive," and be cautious using other criteria, such as neighborhood, credit history, or criminal history, that may have a disparate impact on a protected population. Some states and many locales have "ban the box" laws that prohibit employers from asking about criminal histories on employment applications, although criminal-background checks would later be permissible after offer of hire. The large number of protected categories, and the fact that all of us are members of one or more protected category, together constrain employers to advertise and hire reliably to valid job criteria. You should in other words be getting a fair shake when applying for jobs. Defamation and privacy laws protect you from other unfair recruitment practices. Consult your lawyer whenever you suspect that discrimination or similar foul play is keeping you from getting a job.

Audit: If you have been applying for jobs without success, then consider whether you have evidence that any of the following factors have been preventing your success: (a) your race, ethnicity, ancestry, or national origin; (b) your age; (c) your sex, marital status, family status, or orientation; (d) your health, disability, or genetics; (e) your faith or religion; (f) your height, weight, or appearance; (g) your military service; (h) your citizenship; (i) your criminal history or credit history; (j) false statements from former employers. Consult your lawyer if you have evidence that any of these factors are preventing your employment. **Score [___]**

Available Law Services: investigating and advising you on employer recruitment practices; requesting or demanding that employers stop unlawful recruitment practices; cease-and-desist demands to former employers publishing false information and negotiation for sound references; helping you prepare Equal Employment Opportunity complaints; representing you in administrative and court actions against employers for unlawful recruitment practices.

Your Security

Once you have a job, your first concern is keeping the job, with which the law also has ways to help you. Employers employ the vast majority of U.S. workers *at will*, meaning that the employer may terminate the employment for no reason or any lawful reason. At-will employment offers little job security. Few private employers promise discharge only for good cause. Federal and state labor laws grant workers the right to organize into unions and bargain for job security and other terms. In the small percentage of private jobs where such union labor agreements exist, they routinely provide for discharge from employment only for good cause such as misconduct on the job. Whether your employment is union or non-union makes a job-security difference. Public workers (those working for government) may have job security through civil-service systems, tenure or other laws, and constitutional due-process protections. When it comes to job security, anti-discrimination laws also once again have an influence. The same federal and state laws that protect you against race, sex, religious, age, and other discrimination in hiring also protect you against discriminatory firing. Employers thus tend to document sound reasons for firing of any employee, whether or not employed at will, to avoid discrimination charges. Consult your lawyer any time that you believe that job security should have protected your employment.

Audit: Determine the job security under which you hold your current employment, whether: (a) at will; (b) express or implied contract for termination with cause only; (c) legitimate expectation of continued employment; (d) labor agreement for termination with cause only; (e) public-employee due process notice and hearing before termination; (f) civil servant termination only for wrongful conduct; (g) statutory tenure or similar statutory protection. Consult your lawyer if you are unsure of your job security or face a dispute regarding job security. **Score [___]**

Available Law Services: negotiating job-security terms for your employment; evaluating and advising you on union organizing and bargaining disputes; referring labor disputes for administrative enforcement; investigating, evaluating, representing, and advising you in wrongful-discharge claims; negotiating severance and references; advising and representing you in unemployment-benefits disputes.

Your Wages

Federal and state laws have a lot to say about the amount, form, and timely payment of your wages, all for your benefit. Federal law establishes a minimum hourly wage that many states and locales increase. Employers must pay the highest applicable minimum wage for every hour that covered employees work. Minimum wage laws generally apply to non-supervisory personnel. The same federal and state laws mandate time-and-a-half pay for overtime hours worked in excess of 40 hours per week for the same personnel. Exempt (generally supervisory) personnel do not receive overtime. Know your classification and rights. State laws also require compensation at least monthly for all hours worked in that month. The same laws generally require payment in U.S. currency or equivalent bank check or deposit. State laws prohibit employers from requiring employees to keep their wage secret. Employees may disclose and discuss their wage without employer retaliation. State laws also restrict the deductions and setoffs that employers may make against wages and require notices for allowed deductions and setoffs. Consult your lawyer if you have questions or concerns over whether your employer is paying you lawfully.

Audit: Confirm whether the law mandates overtime pay for your position or whether your position is exempt. If minimum-wage and overtime-pay laws apply to you, then confirm the following: (a) that you are receiving minimum wage; (b) that you are receiving overtime pay when due; (c) that your employer is counting all work hours properly. Whether or not minimum-wage and overtime-pay laws apply to your position, confirm whether you have any disagreement with your employer over: (a) timing of your pay; (b) currency or deposit by which paid; (c) deductions or setoffs from your pay. Consult your lawyer if you have any wage concerns or questions. **Score [___]**

Available Law Services: investigating and confirming your position's status as exempt or non-exempt; investigating and advising you as to which hours to count as work; representing you in wage disputes over minimum wage, overtime pay, or hours worked; reviewing and advising you as to allowable deductions and setoffs from your wage; referring your wage matter for administrative enforcement.

Your Benefits

Federal laws closely regulate your employment benefits. Federal law mandates that employers of 50 or more employees offer health insurance meeting minimum-coverage requirements to employees working at least 30 hours per week. Other federal laws offer you significant tax advantage for employer-provided benefits. For example, employees do not currently pay income taxes on employer health-insurance plans including health savings accounts that comply with federal law. Until the Affordable Care Act takes full effect, you can pay for all qualifying employer-provided healthcare insurance with pre-tax rather than post-tax dollars. The same is true for qualifying employer retirement plans like 401(k), 403(b), and SEP-IRA plans that you can fund them with pre-tax rather than post-tax dollars. Federal law also provides for employers to report to you on the cost of your retirement-plan investments and to insure certain defined-benefit pension plans to protect against employer failure. Federal laws also authorize employers to allow you to choose among healthcare, childcare, and other benefits in what the law refers to as *cafeteria* plans. Federal law simultaneously limits qualifying employer healthcare and retirement plans in the degree to which they can favor one class of employees over another class in those benefits offers. You likely should be receiving benefits like others receive at your place of fulltime employment. When an employer-provided healthcare plan refuses to supply a due benefit, federal law supports your private right of action to recover that benefit. Consult your lawyer when you face employee-benefit issues.

Audit: Identify whether you currently face or soon expect to face any of the following employee-benefit issues: (a) qualifying for health-insurance coverage; (b) dependents qualifying for health-insurance coverage; (c) paying more of the health-insurance premium than you ought to pay; (d) receiving less health-insurance coverage than you ought to receive; (e) not having your health insurance cover a necessary or helpful medical therapy when the insurance should cover it; (f) qualifying for a retirement plan; (g) receiving less of a contribution to your retirement plan than you should receive; (h) undue restrictions on your retirement-plan rollover or investing. Consult your lawyer if you face these or similar employee-benefit issues. **Score [___]**

Available Law Services: reviewing and advising you as to your employee benefits; negotiating with your employer for benefits; representing you in disputes with your employer over your qualification for or scope of benefits; representing you in disputes with your health insurer over covered services.

Your Records

Federal and state laws require employers to keep certain records of your employment while giving you access to those records. If your employment is so important to you (as we know it is), then you should have access to what your employer documents about it. Employment laws covering all sorts of subjects like wages, benefits, leaves, exposures, injuries, and discrimination require your employer to retain records. For example, if your employment exposed you to toxic chemicals, then federal and state occupational-safety laws require your employer to retain those exposure records for decades. If you reported harassment or discrimination, then equal-employment-opportunity laws require your employer to save those records for a period of at least three years. Your employer must be able to produce payroll records to document and prove that it paid minimum wage and overtime pay, workplace-injury reports to address safety and worker's compensation issues, and attendance records to document compliance with medical-leave and family-leave laws. Federal and state laws require that employers keep certain records confidential unless notifying you before disclosure and in some instances obtaining your consent. State laws in some states prohibit employers from keeping records of your political affiliation and restrict your employer from disclosing your Social Security number. Other laws require employers to keep your personnel records in one place but to segregate and maintain as confidential medical records relating to your employment. State laws require that your employer share your personnel records with you and allow you to challenge and dispute their accuracy, while also requiring your employer to copy them for you on your request. Consult your lawyer if you disagree with your employer over access to or content of your personnel records.

Audit: Which of your following personal information does your employer have in your personnel records? (a) Academic transcript. (b) Psychological profile. (c) Personality profile. (d) Intelligence test scores. (e) Credit record and score. (f) Criminal history. (g) Driving record. (h) Medical history. (i) Social Security number. (j) Bank and savings or checking account number. (k) Marital history. (l) Names, ages, and Social Security numbers of children. (m) Payroll history. (n) Retirement-account broker and number. (o) Emergency contact name and number. (p) Work-discipline history. (q) Work evaluations. Where does your employer keep this information, and who has access to it? Consult your lawyer if you have experienced an embarrassing or concerning disclosure of employment information, or your employment information is inaccurate, and your employer will not address your concerns. **Score [___]**

Available Law Services: advising you as to your personnel records; obtaining a copy of your personnel record for you; representing you in demanding correction or redaction of your personnel records.

Your Accommodation

Federal and state laws require employers to provide reasonable accommodations so that physical and mental disabilities do not prevent qualified employee from doing their job. These laws interpret broadly the kind of disabilities employers must reasonably accommodate. Obvious orthopedic impairments like a bad arm, leg, or back can qualify as protected disabilities if you could do the job with reasonable accommodation of that impairment, while less-obvious neurological, pulmonary, psychological, and other impairing disorders can also qualify. The laws also interpret broadly the kind of accommodations the employer must supply. As long as the accommodation does not work an employer undue hardship, the employer may among other things have to provide ramps, lifts, and other physical aids, modify sound and lighting, provide sign language for the hearing impaired and text readers for the visually impaired, and make schedule changes. Employers must work with you and vocational experts in a flexible interactive process to ensure that disabilities do not prevent you from performing a job that with reasonable accommodation you could perform. Consult your lawyer if you are experiencing difficulties performing your work that you could perform with reasonable accommodation, and your employer is not cooperating.

Audit: Do you have any physical or mental impairments that interfere with major life functions? If so, then do they affect your work? Could you perform your work better if your employer provided you with a reasonable accommodation of that impairment? What would that accommodation be? Consult your lawyer about these issues. **Score [___]**

Available Law Services: investigating, evaluating, and advising you as to your rights to reasonable accommodation; referring your matter for administrative enforcement; representing you in an action against your employer to compel reasonable accommodation.

Your Leave

Federal law guarantees qualifying employees up to 12 weeks of medical leave per year for a serious health condition or leave to care for a family member with a serious health condition, from employers employing 50 or more employees within a 75-mile radius of your job site. The law also protects leave for pregnancy, infant care, and adoption, and extends the 12 weeks to 26 weeks when the care is for an injured service-member. You must notify the employer in advance or as soon as reasonably possible of your need for leave. The employer must notify you of your leave rights and that it is counting certain absences as leave days against your allowed 12 weeks per year. Your leave time may be intermittent and for different conditions. A serious health condition is one for which you were hospitalized overnight or for which medical care providers treated you at least twice. To be eligible for leave, you must have worked for the employer at least 1,250 hours in the prior year and must have worked for the employer a total of at least 12 months. You must supply medical certification of your need for leave, and your employer may require a second or third opinion. On your return to work, the employer must return you to your pre-leave job or one nearly identical but may require you to submit to a fitness-for-duty examination. While law does not require that your employer pay you wages for your leave time, your employer must continue health-insurance benefits. Consult your lawyer if you have disputes with your employer over protected leave time.

Audit: Have you taken or do you expect to take medical or family leave from your employment this year? If so, then confirm the following information: (a) whether your employer is large enough that it must comply with federal employment-leave laws; (b) whether you have worked long enough for your employer to qualify for leave; (c) what forms and certifications your employer requires; (d) whether your leave days will approach 12 weeks; (e) the one-year period that your employer uses to count the 12 weeks. Consult your lawyer if you cannot determine this information or obtain it from your employer. **Score [___]**

Available Law Services: evaluating and advising you as to your medical-leave rights; communicating with your employer to confirm and document your leave rights; representing you in an action to enforce your federal employment-leave rights.

Your Safety

Federal and state occupational-safety laws closely regulate your workplace to protect you from injury. Those laws authorize detailed regulations covering specific workplace activities within specific industries. Depending on the type of work employees perform, your employer may have to comply with federal and state regulations governing hazardous materials, warnings, guarding, protective clothing and equipment, processes, ingress and egress, environmental exposures, noise levels, lighting levels, and other conditions and aspects of your work. When specific safety regulations do not address your work, a general-safety regulation requires that your employer keep your workplace free from recognized hazards likely to cause serious injury. State regulators enforce these occupational-safety requirements through an administrative system that threatens violating employers with fines, stop-work orders, and even criminal charges. Occupational-safety laws also require employers to report serious workplace injuries and to make those reports available to employees so that you know the safety issues in your workplace. State safety inspectors make scheduled inspections, surprise inspections, and injury investigations, to keep your workplace reasonably safe. The law prohibits employers from retaliating against you for reporting unsafe workplace conditions. Consult your lawyer if you encounter serious safety concerns in the workplace that your employer is not addressing.

Audit: Which of the following safety concerns do you face in your workplace? (a) Dangerous presses, die-cast machines, or other manufacturing equipment. (b) Dangerous conveyors, lifts, or other materials-handling equipment. (c) Caustic or toxic chemicals. (d) Unassisted hand movement of heavy items. (e) Repetitive-motion hazards. (f) Slippery floors and other surfaces. (g) Working from ladders, lifts, or other heights. (h) Dust, smoke, or other breathing hazards. (i) Loud or constant noise. (j) High-speed drills, abrasive wheels, or other rotating equipment.

Consult your lawyer if your employer is not addressing these or other safety concerns. **Score [___]**

Available Law Services: helping you notify and negotiate with your employer over safety issues; helping you obtain and review workplace injury and exposure reports; helping you report workplace-safety issues to state officials; representing you in employer-retaliation claims; advising and representing you over workplace injuries.

Your Injury

State worker's compensation laws guarantee compensation for your workplace injury. If you suffer unintentional injury in the course of your employment, then your employer or its insurer should pay for related reasonably necessary medical expense and a substantial percentage of your wage loss as state law determines. Worker's compensation is a no-fault system, meaning that you receive the benefits whether or not you or your employer were at fault, but you may not sue your employer or co-workers for negligence to recover other economic or non-economic losses. Depending on your state's law and the particular injury circumstances, you may not receive benefits if you intended your own injury or, in some cases, if your actions were due to your own drunkenness or other misconduct unrelated to work. To qualify for worker's compensation benefits, you must ordinarily be able to attribute your injury to a specific traumatic workplace event. Worker's compensation does not ordinarily pay for chronic degenerative conditions, although worker's compensation will often cover certain occupational diseases. Worker's compensation is an administrative system, meaning that disputes over claims and benefits go before administrative tribunals rather than general-jurisdiction courts. While employers must insure for or otherwise guarantee worker's compensation benefits, which is often a costly business expense depending on injury and claim rates, employers must also not retaliate against employees who seek worker's compensation benefits. Consult your lawyer about these rights if you suffer a serious workplace injury.

Audit: If you have suffered a workplace injury, then confirm the following, that: (a) no one intended your injury; (b) no one other than you, your employer, and your co-workers was responsible for your injury; (c) comp paid all of your medical expenses; (d) comp paid the statutory percentage of your wage loss; (e) you were due no additional specific-loss benefit for amputation or permanent loss of use; (f) your employer restored you to your job after your recovery; (g) your employer did not retaliate for your comp claim in any other way; (h) you have completed your recovery with all rehabilitation services that you need; (i) you have no remaining work disability from your workplace injury. Consult your lawyer if you have any question over these or related circumstances relating to your worker's compensation rights and benefits. **Score [____]**

Available Law Services: investigating and obtaining records of your workplace injury; advising you on your worker's compensation rights; communicating with your employer or its insurer over worker's compensation claims and benefits; representing you in worker's compensation administrative claims.

Your Termination

Because job loss has such serious financial and other consequences, federal and state laws provide you with certain protections. If you had your employer's promise of continued employment, then you may have a claim against your employer for wrongful discharge. If you were a union member, then you may have the right to grieve your discharge and obtain reinstatement. If your discharge was unlawfully discriminatory or retaliatory, then you would have a private right of action for damages and reinstatement. If your discharge was part of a qualifying mass layoff or plant closure, then federal law would require your employer to give you 60-day notice. Even if your employer had the legal right to terminate your employment, under state wage laws it must pay your wages timely. Your employer may also owe you unemployment benefits. Firing alone does not disqualify you from unemployment benefits. State laws disqualify workers who deliberately disregard their employer's significant interests, more in the nature of willful misconduct than mistake, lack of productivity or fit, or even incompetence. Your employer may also be willing to pay you severance voluntarily. Federal law requires that your employer notify you of your right (known as COBRA rights) to continue your group health insurance at your expense. Federal law also protects your right to control and rollover your 401(k) retirement account. Your greatest interest, though, may be in securing a reliable recommendation letter and personal reference from your former employer because at the moment of your job termination your next job becomes more important than your last one. Consult your lawyer about these important rights in the event of your job loss.

Audit: If you have recently lost a job or about to do so, then confirm that you have addressed to your satisfaction each of the following issues: (a) the grounds for your job termination; (b) whether those grounds were unlawfully discriminatory or retaliatory; (c) whether your termination was part of a mass layoff or plant closing and, if so, then whether you had 60-day notice; (d) full payment of your last wage; (e) any severance pay your employer is willing to pay; (f) continuation of your health insurance; (g) whether you qualify for unemployment benefits; (h) your employer's recommendation letter and reference; (i) your rollover and other control of your employer retirement account. Consult your lawyer if you have questions or concerns over any of these or similar issues that your employer is not addressing. Score [___]

Available Law Services: investigating the legal grounds for your termination; helping you obtain a copy of your employment file; referring you for administrative enforcement of your claim for last wages; negotiating severance benefits, recommendation letter, and reference; representing you in wrongful-discharge or discrimination claims; representing you in unemployment claims.

7 Your Family

Families mean so much to our health and welfare, and that of American society, that law would naturally have a lot to say about them. The things most important to us occur within families, from birth through infancy, education and maturation, love and intimacy, homemaking, sickness, disability, and mourning death. The laws that preserve, protect, and promote families are primarily state laws, although federal laws increasingly affect family issues like domestic-violence prevention, interstate child-support enforcement, division of retirement plans in divorce, and of course household income taxes. Family laws become critical when families are in crisis, but even in stable and secure times you can benefit by knowing and pursuing the benefits and protections of family laws. Consider the following sections on the laws of cohabitation, marriage, divorce, children, and other family laws. Know your family rights, responsibilities, and opportunities.

Your Cohabiting

Before we consider the laws of marriage, first consider the laws affecting persons who live together without marrying. The laws of cohabitation are not truly specific to cohabitants. Marriage and divorce laws provide frameworks for the rights and responsibilities of persons who marry. The legislatures and courts have been reluctant to develop any equivalent set of laws governing the rights and responsibilities of non-married cohabitants. While states have alimony (spousal support) laws governing obligations between divorcing spouses, states do not recognize equivalent so-called *palimony* rights for separating non-married cohabitants even when the cohabitation has been long, close, and stable. Instead, cohabitants must rely on general property law, contract law, tort law, and other general laws, fitting them to the cohabitation circumstance. Because law offers no particularly well-developed legal framework for cohabitation, some cohabitants are entering into cohabitation agreements. Cohabitation agreements are simply contracts that provide a framework of mutual rights and obligations around subjects like home ownership and maintenance, personal-property ownership, financial support of one another whether in health or disability, household services, control of accounts, care for children and pets, and temporary or permanent separation. One way of looking at the subject is that from a legal standpoint, cohabitation can take more thought and planning than marriage takes, where rights and obligations are clearer. Do not underestimate the significance of the property, financial, support, services, and other issues that cohabitation can create. Consult your lawyer before you face cohabitation issues in the midst of crisis. Let law help you order your relationships.

Audit: If you are cohabiting or considering doing so, then rank your greatest unaddressed concerns from among the following: (a) ownership, use, and maintenance of, and payment for, the residence; (b) ownership of, access to, and benefit from bank, brokerage, and retirement accounts; (c) ownership, use, and maintenance of, and payment for, vehicles; (d) support, care, and custody of children; (e) ownership, care, and custody of pets; (f) ownership of home electronics, recreational equipment, art, and other valuable personal property; (g) ownership, control, and use of kitchen and home appliances, linens, and other household effects; (h) financial support of one another whether in sickness or in health; (i) payment of joint credit cards or other loans and

debts. Consult your lawyer to help you address those concerns.
Score [___]

Available Law Services: providing you with a cohabitation agreement; representing you in negotiating a cohabitation agreement; helping you mediate and resolve cohabitation disputes; defending or pursuing a court action preserving your property and contract rights after cohabitation.

Your Marriage

As the prior section on cohabitation intimates, the laws of marriage provide a framework for persons living together in long-term union and intimacy. Legislatures enact and courts interpret those laws to promote marriage. State laws define what constitutes marriage, typically requiring a license, ceremony, and consummation between two competent, consenting, and not-currently married adults. States may impose other requirements to obtain the license, such as residency within the state for some period, waiting period, vaccination, blood testing particularly for venereal disease (less common today), and proof of lawful termination of prior marriages. Spouses, particularly the wife, need not but may take the last name of the other. In the event of divorce, the divorce judgment will provide whether a spouse who had changed a name at marriage has elected to restore the maiden name used before marriage. State laws no longer recognize common-law marriages (living together claiming marriage but without the requisite license and ceremony), although many states did so at one time, and some very long-term common-law marriages survive. State laws provide that marriage gives you certain rights such as the right of your spouse's support, sometimes called the *necessaries* doctrine. Some states extend that obligation to mean that one spouse must pay for the healthcare of the other spouse, making both spouses liable to unpaid care providers. Generally, though, one spouse is not liable for the other spouse's individual debts unless expressly acknowledging the debt such as on a joint credit card. Indeed, one of the greater financial protections of marriage is that property held together in marriage (known as *entireties* property) is exempt from execution by judgment creditors of either individual spouse. Marriage can also mean lower marginal income-tax rates for joint filers if one spouse earns all or most of the household income. On the other hand, if both of you earn about the same, then the marginal tax rates can be higher (known as the *marriage penalty*). Marriage affords dozens of other advantages around retirement plans, insurance plans, Social Security, inheritance, property rights, separation, divorce, and other important subjects. Some marrying couples enter into prenuptial (also called *antenuptial*) agreements to modify some of those legal rights. Spouses are not liable for the misconduct or carelessness, or responsible for the crimes, of the other. Under certain conditions, they also have privileges not to testify against one another and to keep confidential private communications made between them during the marriage. Consult your lawyer if you wish to know more about your rights, obligations, and opportunities within marriage.

Audit: If you are married, then how do you hold and designate your accounts, insurances, and properties? Confirm that you hold joint savings and checking accounts, have designated each other as beneficiaries on any life insurance or retirement accounts, and are both on your home's deed as spouses, but that you keep separate titles and registrations to your vehicles and, if creditworthiness is any issue, then also separate consumer loans and credit cards. If you are contemplating marriage, then consider planning and preparing for the same. **Score [___]**

Available Law Services: researching and advising you on your state's laws of marriage; helping you obtain court judgments and orders necessary for a marriage license; representing you in drafting a prenuptial agreement; helping you title property by the entireties to protect it against execution; defending your entireties property against execution by sole creditors; advocating your marriage rights and benefits with insurers and government agencies; advocating your marriage rights in contested estate proceedings.

Your Divorce

Just as the law provides marriage terms, the law also provides the terms on which marriages end whether by annulment or divorce. Divorce law is state law, meaning that it varies somewhat from state to state. States generally have residency requirements varying from 30 days to one year to obtain a divorce within the state plus a waiting period of days or months between filing for divorce and obtaining a divorce judgment. Many states provide for no-fault divorce, meaning that only one spouse need attest that the marriage is irretrievably broken and wait the statutory period to obtain a divorce judgment ending the marriage. Other states give an option of no-fault or fault-based divorce including grounds like cruelty, adultery, or abandonment, proof of which may affect how the court divides property or assigns spousal support (alimony). Property division and spousal support are substantial issues in divorce. (See below for children issues.) State laws vary but tend to start with a presumption that divorcing spouses divide marital assets and debts equally, with adjustments reflecting many factors including each party's ability to provide that party's own support, which is also a primary factor, along with income, education, and length of the marriage, for whether the court will require either party to support the other after divorce. Marital assets are generally those accumulated during the marriage other than by gift or inheritance. Courts usually enter divorce judgments by consent after the parties agree to terms but sometimes must impose the judgment. State laws usually permit annulments instead of divorce only when one of the parties was already and still married (meaning the new marriage was unlawfully bigamous), one of the parties coerced or defrauded the other party, one of the parties is under the age of consent, and in instances where the parties have not yet consummated the marriage. States also recognize formal separations short of complete divorce, giving separated parties access to the courts to help decide property and support issues. Consult your lawyer for more information on separation and divorce.

Audit: If you or your spouse are contemplating separation or divorce, then identify which of the following issues you have considered: (a) marriage counseling; (b) reconciliation; (c) mediation; (d) property division; (e) division of debts; (f) division of retirement accounts; (g) spousal support; (h) who retains the marital home; (i) if children, then child custody and support; (j) who retains pets; (k) representation; (l) place and timing of filing court action. Consult your lawyer if you have questions regarding these and other issues relating to divorce or separation. **Score [___]**

Available Law Services: advising you regarding the laws of marriage, separation, and divorce; providing and preparing divorce forms and instructions; mediating reconciliation, separation, or divorce issues between you and your spouse; representing you in a divorce action; moving to enforce your divorce judgment after its entry.

Your Children

The law obviously governs many important rights and responsibilities regarding your children. Knowing the law can help you pursue the best interests of your children. The law first addresses who are your children, particularly when you have children outside of marriage. Paternity actions brought by the mother or the state will establish, often by blood test but sometimes by testimony or default, who is a child's father, following which the father will have the support obligations and may have the parenting rights of a father. While state laws tend to promote and protect child-rearing within marriage by presuming that children born during the marriage are children of the marriage, states may recognize a husband's opportunity to dispute paternity and disavow parentage before acknowledgment. Be aware: state procedures for establishing, disproving, or disavowing parentage are strict and can be complex. When parentage is established, state laws respect broad parental rights to raise, supervise, instruct, and provide for children without the interference of others or of the state. State laws also permit you to designate temporary guardians over your children while you are incapacitated or away. You may also in your will recommend permanent guardians in the event of your death. Parents lose those parental rights for abuse and neglect but only after notice and court hearing. Parents who live apart must either agree on physical and legal custody of children or have a court decide based on factors including fitness, safety, and support. Joint legal custody where both parents together make major decisions regarding the child is common, while joint physical custody may also be possible with the child dividing time between households. Otherwise, the non-custodial parent will have parenting time (visitation rights) unless a court has safety or other reasons not to allow it. Non-custodial parents pay child support based on the relative income of each parent. Courts can enforce child support with contempt sanctions including incarceration. Consult your lawyer when facing these or similar issues relating to your children.

Audit: Identify which if any of the following concerns do you have affecting the health, welfare, or other best interests of your child or children: (a) paternity; (b) legal custody; (c) physical custody; (d) support; (e) parenting time; (f) support arrearages; (g) abuse; (h) neglect; (i) safety; (j) temporary guardianship; (k) permanent guardianship. Consult your lawyer to address any of those concerns. **Score [___]**

Available Law Services: advising you on paternity laws; representing you in paternity actions; advising you on parental rights; representing you in actions to preserve and pursue parental rights; helping you establish or preserve child custody; helping you pursue child support and support enforcement; helping you modify custody, parenting-time and child-support orders as circumstances change; helping you collect child-support arrearages.

Your Youth

The law affords children greater rights as they mature while also holding them increasingly responsible, a transition with which you may help your child maturing through youth. Youth rights include eventual emancipation, meaning the legal right at least by adulthood to decide where and with whom to live, where to attend schooling, and other major and minor decisions regarding health, education, and welfare. Even as to child custody, as children mature into their teens, judges are more likely to consider the child's own expressed interest as to which separated or divorced parent with whom to live. State laws provide for ages when a child's minority becomes an adult's majority for various purposes relating to independent decision-making. Depending on the state, that age is often 18 years of age (for example, for hazardous work or for entering into binding contracts) but for some purposes as young as age 16 (for example, for consensual sex, marriage, or motor-vehicle driving) and for other purposes age 21 (for example, for drinking alcohol or smoking). Yet states permit minors to petition the courts to lower the age of emancipation for some purposes, for example for living apart from parents. Juvenile law rather than criminal law judges youth misconduct. Juveniles have the advantage of confidential proceedings and records, and special detentions that end typically in freedom when the detained juvenile reaches adulthood. Minors engaging in conduct reserved for adults may face criminal charge or juvenile sanction (as minors in possession of alcohol, for instance), while adults who assist those minors may face criminal charges (for instance, statutory rape for sex with an underage minor). Law may permit a court to reduce the age at which the court judges a youth under adult criminal laws, sometimes to as young as age 12 or 13. Some states hold parents civilly liable for willful or reckless injury, loss, or damage that their children cause but limit that liability to a specific figure such as $5,000.

Audit: If you have a child maturing through youth or are responsible for such a child, then confirm whether any of the following are concerns or issues for that child: (a) custodial parents; (b) emancipation; (c) underage work; (d) underage marriage; (e) drinking alcohol; (f) smoking; (g) use of illicit drugs; (h) underage sex; (i) teen pregnancy; (j) association with adults engaged in criminal conduct. Consult your lawyer about any of these subjects that are issues for your youth. **Score [___]**

Available Law Services: representing you or your youth in emancipation proceedings; petitioning to approve that your youth engage in adult activities; representing youth in a juvenile proceeding; defending youth against criminal charges; negotiating pleas and sentences that preserve a youth's future record; acting as guardian ad litem to evaluate and advocate on your youth's behalf.

Your Care

As the above section on marriage indicates, spouses owe one another the duty of support for necessary items such as food, clothing, and shelter. State laws further provide that spouses owe one another duties of love, society, services, and sexual intimacy, and fiduciary duties in financial transactions. Your spouse should serve and support you, just as you should serve and support your spouse. A third-party wrongdoer who injures one spouse in a way that prevents the injured spouse from fulfilling those duties will owe the other (uninjured) spouse *consortium-loss* damages along with the damages that the wrongdoer would owe the injured spouse. State laws once recognized alienation-of-affection claims against third parties whose successful solicitation of one spouse's affections disrupted the marital rights of the other spouse, but states have generally abandoned such claims. Spouses also owe duties of reasonable care to one another, meaning that if one's negligence injures the other, the injured spouse may be due compensation from the negligent spouse. A few states grant inter-spousal immunity from one another's negligence suits, but other states do not, and many states provide numerous exceptions where suits between spouses may proceed for things like motor-vehicle-accident injuries, assault and battery, and intentional infliction of emotional distress, or when divorced. This inter-spousal remedy would make little sense for spouses who live together and share finances but more sense where liability insurance would pay for injuries due to negligence. Some state statutes require adult children to provide necessities for the support of an aged parent who is unable to provide his or her own support, but states seldom enforce those statutes. States may also criminalize an adult child's knowing neglect to care for a dependent resident aged and infirm parent, but again, seldom with enforcement. Under some circumstances, particularly when a child is involved or the spouse is elderly, Social Security disability benefits extend to the disabled person's dependent spouse. Consult your lawyer when you have questions over obligations of intra-family support.

Audit: Identify whether you have any of the following concerns or disagreements, or face any of the following issues, having to do with family support: (a) your support by a spouse; (b) your support of a spouse; (c) your support by an adult child; (d) your support of an aged and infirm parent; (e) your liability for necessary goods or services supplied to your spouse; (f) your spouse's liability for necessary goods or services supplied to you.

Consult your lawyer over each identified intra-family support concern. **Score [___]**

Available Law Services: advising you regarding your right to support from spouse or adult children; advising you regarding your obligation to support spouse or aged and infirm parents; representing you in an action for support from or to your spouse; defending you in actions by third parties for necessities supplied to your spouse; representing you in a negligence suit against your spouse for liability-insurance recovery; representing you for consortium loss when a third party injures your spouse; advising you regarding Social Security disability benefits owing to the claimant's spouse.

Your Dying

Just as the law helps you with the rights and obligations of care while living within a family, so too does the law help you with the process of dying within a family. Guardianships, conservatorships, and healthcare powers of attorney, and advance directives (otherwise known as living wills) are four tools that the law authorizes to provide you and others with guidance as you become less able to make decisions for yourself. State laws regulate the procedures and forms for all four tools. A guardianship designates a trusted person, usually your spouse, adult child, or other family member, to make decisions about your physical care such as where you will live and what services you will receive when you can no longer make those decisions for yourself. For effect, guardianships usually require a probate or family court order. Conservatorships are similar except that they designate a person to care for your legal and financial affairs rather you're your physical needs. The same person often but not always serves as guardian and conservator. A durable power of attorney for healthcare is a document that you may execute at any time, authorizing a trusted family member or other person to direct your medical care providers if you suddenly become unable to do so. An advance directive or living will is a document in which you tell your guardian and care providers what medical, palliative, and resuscitative care to provide in your terminal illness or other last days. Together, the four tools of guardianship, conservatorship, healthcare powers, and advance directives create a legal framework within which you can die in greater grace, with less confusion, disagreement, or uncertainty over your person and affairs. The elderly also often execute legal and financial powers of attorney to enable a trusted adult child to manage or share in managing their affairs even though they remain competent. After death, law requires a designated professional to examine the body and complete a certificate of death before the body's release and final disposition according to your instructions. State laws also regulate the handling and cremation, interment, or other disposition of the body including autopsy and organ donation. Consult your lawyer if you have questions or concerns, and when you are prepared to give directions, regarding your dying.

Audit: Identify whether you or anyone for whom you have responsibility needs the following relating to serious or terminal illness or other approaching potential demise: (a) guardianship because of declining ability to make decisions about physical security, safety, and care; (b) conservatorship because of increasing incompetence to make sound legal and financial decisions; (c) power of attorney to assist in managing legal and financial affairs; (d) durable power of attorney for healthcare decisions to manage long-term physical care; (e) patient designate to make healthcare decisions during surgery under general anesthetic; (f) advance directive regarding medical and palliative care for terminal illness. Consult your lawyer to discuss and meet any of these needs. **Score [___]**

Available Law Services: providing healthcare durable powers of attorney; providing financial durable powers of attorney; drafting advance medical directives; helping you or your family members obtain guardianship and conservatorship orders.

8 Your Finances

Your finances have a lot to do with how well you manage your life for your own benefit and the benefit of those around you. Other things tend not to work so well when your finances are poor or disordered. The law has a lot to say to protect and manage your finances. When you need the help of financial institutions to manage your finances responsibly, law regulates those institutions and your relationship with them. When you need to borrow money for a home, vehicle, or other purpose, the law regulates the lender and lending. When you have debt problems, the law regulates the collection of that debt. Law also regulates checking, savings, and retirement accounts. Then, we have the law of taxes including income, sales, real-property, and other taxes. Know the laws affecting your finances while putting those laws to good uses to keep your finances in order.

Your Banking

Financial institutions are a virtual necessity in today's modern economy. Prospering without a bank through which to conduct financial transactions is difficult. Federal and state laws regulate banks closely to ensure the security of your funds and your fair treatment. A federal program insures your bank deposits up to

$250,000 per account. Banks control access to your account through your account agreement, which is the contract that you sign when opening the account. That contract may take the form of a signature card that both identifies your signature for security purposes and includes the terms on which the bank will handle your funds. State contract law, the law of negotiable instruments, and federal banking regulations then together ensure that banks handle your accounts and transactions responsibly according to the terms of your account agreement. When, for instance, a bank releases account funds over a signature that you have not authorized, state law would ordinarily require that the bank restore the funds, particularly if you are monitoring your account statements to notify the bank timely of any irregularity. No one other than you and those whom you designate should control your funds, for instance for direct withdrawal, except as law may otherwise provide. The account agreement will also control what fees the bank may charge you for transactions and services. When banks fail to disclose fees and charges properly, or otherwise mislead customers as to the cost and nature of their services, state law and federal regulations provide you with remedies. Banks are not perfect, and they are also not always perfectly honest. Consult your lawyer when you face banking issues over excessive or undisclosed fees and charges, loss of your funds, product or service misrepresentations, and other irregularities.

Audit: For each of your bank accounts, whether checking, savings, or other, determine and document in a single place the following information: (a) the banking institution; (b) the type of account; (c) all persons whom you have granted access to the account; (d) all persons who hold an interest in the account whether or not they have access; (e) all periodic obligations (car-loan payments, utility-bill payment, etc.) that you have authorized the bank to pay automatically; (f) the day each month and manner (paper or electronic) in which you receive account statements; (g) your diligent practice of reviewing those statements within a reasonable time after receipt. Consult your lawyer if you discover

86

any irregularity or issue in the handling or security of your bank accounts. **Score [___]**

Available Law Services: reviewing and advising you as to account agreements; obtaining and reconciling account statements for you; reviewing and advising you as to account statements and transactions; advocating for you over excessive or undisclosed fees; referring your matters to bank regulators; representing you in actions against your bank to restore lost funds or gain promised services.

Your Borrowing

Federal credit-reporting laws give you the right to dispute and correct inaccurate credit reports to ensure that you have a fair chance at obtaining credit. Lenders must notify you when they use a credit report to deny you credit. Federal and state law also regulate consumer lending to protect you against misleading and unfair practices. Borrowing is a matter of state contract law governing the terms between borrower and lender. Lenders must disclose and borrowers must agree to the material terms of the loans including the loan amount, loan duration including any balloon payment or other acceleration, interest rate, and whether the rate is fixed or floating. Yet consumer loans like credit cards, home mortgages, home-equity lines of credit, and vehicle financing all must also comply with federal and state truth-in-lending laws and regulations that prohibit unfair and deceptive lending practices. Those laws and regulations require the above disclosures of loan terms while also requiring disclosure of loan costs that enable consumers to compare costs. Truth-in-lending laws also require disclosures of fees and late charges, give consumers three days to rescind the loan agreement at no cost, and require accurate billing. Regulations also limit the amount of the penalty fees that consumer lenders may charge for a first late payment and subsequent late payments. Other credit laws and regulations prohibit discrimination in housing and consumer lending based on race, sex, religion, disability, marital status, and family status, while also prohibiting predatory lending taking unfair advantage of minorities, the undereducated, non-English speakers, and economically oppressed. Consult your lawyer if you believe that your lender has engaged in an unfair, deceptive, or discriminatory practice, is charging excessive fees, or is not keeping accurate records of your loan balance.

Audit: For each consumer loan that you are considering or that you owe, determine the following: (a) current administrator of the loan; (b) loan principal owing; (c) current interest rate; (d) whether the rate is fixed or floating; (e) current monthly payment; (f) any anticipated changes in monthly payment; (g) remaining term to payoff; (h) any acceleration or balloon payment including date and amount; (i) any fees or charges assessed and the date and reason. Consult your lawyer if you have any questions or concerns regarding your loan terms, loan accounts, and loan balances. **Score [___]**

Available Law Services: obtaining your credit report for you, and helping you challenge and correct inaccurate reports; reviewing and advising you as to loan terms, and helping you comparison shop; obtaining, reconciling, challenging, and correcting your loan account statements; researching and challenging allowable penalty fees; investigating and representing you relating to discriminatory and predatory lending.

Your Debt

In the event that you fall behind and default on a loan, federal and state laws help ensure your fair treatment in debt collection. Federal and state debt-collection laws prohibit debt collectors from harassing or deceiving you to collect on those debts. Those laws restrict debt collectors to calling you during reasonable hours, to contact only your attorney when they know that an attorney represents you, and to cease communications with you and sue instead when you demand it in writing. You may demand that the debt collector verify the debt. Debt collectors must not make misrepresentations or use deception such as pretending to be lawyers or law-enforcement officials. They must not use profane or abusive language and must not communicate about your debt with third parties like your neighbors or employer. Federal and state debt-relief programs address defaults in home and educational loans, about which debt collectors may have to inform you. The law permits creditors to sue you for your debt and obtain a civil judgment against you. As long as you comply with court orders such as to appear and answer questions about your assets, state laws ordinarily permit creditors to enforce civil judgments by garnishment of your bank accounts and wages or by execution on your non-exempt assets, not by arrest and incarceration. State laws limit wage garnishment to only a portion of your wage, intending to leave you wages on which to live. State laws exempt certain kinds and amounts of real and personal property from execution so that you are not left without any property. Social Security and retirement accounts are ordinarily also exempt. Federal bankruptcy laws permit you to discharge (not pay) certain debts under certain conditions while requiring you to relinquish security for debts and non-exempt assets, and under wage-earner plans to make debt payments for a period of years. Consult your lawyer about these substantial protections when unable to pay your debt.

Audit: If you owe loans that you cannot presently pay, then determine the following: (a) current principal balance on each loan; (b) current monthly minimum payment on each loan; (c) total of all loan balances; (d) total of all monthly minimum payments on all loans; (e) maximum amount you are able to pay on loans each month out of your monthly income after other necessary expenses; (f) name, address, telephone, and email of each entity currently servicing each of your loans; (g) savings or cash you can raise to payoff delinquent loans; (h) payoff amount in delinquency that each loan holder will accept; (i) any practices that any debt collector has engaged in that may violate the above-mentioned laws or otherwise be abusive or deceptive. Consult your lawyer regarding your plan to address your loans in delinquency. **Score [___]**

Available Law Services: advising you regarding your rights in debt collection; representing you in negotiations over settling debts; defending you in debt-collection actions; moving for an order for installment payments on money judgments; representing you in actions against debt collectors who engage in unlawful debt-collection practices; challenging garnishments and execution on exempt assets; representing you in bankruptcy.

Your Investing

Federal and state laws govern the transactions you make when investing, regulate the financial professionals and institutions assisting you with your investing, and create the legal framework for the securities in which you invest. When you buy stock, you buy ownership of a company under state corporate law in a transaction that state and federal securities regulations govern. Securities laws require regulatory filings and public disclosures whenever companies make public offerings of stock to potential investors. Companies having shares traded on exchanges must meet additional regulations. The effect of those regulations is to ensure that the information you and your advisors receive about those companies is accurate and not misleading and that investors trade with the same public information. When you buy bonds, you are loaning money to a corporate or government entity. Bond offerings and markets face similar regulation. Financial advisors whom you retain to help you invest owe you duties of knowledge, skill, care, and loyalty. Advisors who engage in excessive transactions to earn undue fees, sell you inappropriate investments, or otherwise violate their fiduciary duties may owe civil liability or restitution. Sound investing requires knowledge of tax laws such as taxes on capital gains, the tax-free status of certain municipal bonds, and the tax-favored status of certain educational-savings accounts and retirement accounts. You should also be holding your investments in account forms and designating account beneficiaries and secondary beneficiaries in ways that will accomplish your estate-planning goals in the event of your demise. You may benefit from holding certain investments in a trust or conveying certain investments to others now rather than later. Know the legal framework for investments and laws of investing. Consult your lawyer whenever you have concerns or questions regarding the obligations of the companies and agencies issuing securities, duties of financial advisors, and proper handling of your investments.

Audit: Which of the following prudential tasks relating to your investments are you able and willing to perform? (a) Confirming that your financial advisor has the required licenses and recommended certifications. (b) Checking whether regulators have disciplined your financial advisor for misconduct. (c) Confirming the account-beneficiary designations on your accounts. (d) Confirming whether accounts are federally insured. (e) Confirming your financial advisor's fees and charges. Consult your lawyer if you have concerns or questions over these or other investment-practices issues. **Score [___]**

Available Law Services: researching and advising you as to financial-advisor licenses and certifications; reviewing and advising you as to annuity contracts, life-insurance policies, and other investment agreements; reviewing, evaluating, and advising you as to your investment rights and claims; referring your complaints to federal and state securities regulators; representing you in civil actions to recover for misrepresented investments; representing you in civil actions to recover from financial advisors breaching duties.

Your Retirement

We rightly value providing for ourselves in retirement when we are no longer able to earn substantial income. When we do not plan for retirement, the financial burden falls on family members and the public. Laws therefore support our efforts to save for retirement while laws also authorize public retirement and assistance programs and their funding whether or not we succeed in our own efforts. Federal laws create a program for employers to insure defined-benefit pensions. Federal law also authorizes employers to offer the much more common 401(k) defined-contribution retirement plans (known as 403(b) plans for nonprofit workers and 457 plans for government workers). These tax-favored plans allow you to contribute pre-tax dollars, providing you with one substantial financial benefit, and then exempt the earnings from taxation, providing you with another substantial financial benefit, although you do pay taxes at the time of withdrawals. With certain exceptions, federal law penalizes early withdrawals before age 59 ½ and then requires withdrawals beginning at age 70 ½. Federal law also authorizes Roth IRA accounts to which you may contribute post-tax dollars but on which you do not pay taxes on the earnings or withdrawals. Americans have saved trillions of retirement dollars using these programs. Federal law requires that employees and employers together pay Social Security and Medicare taxes totaling 15.3% of wages, over and above federal, state, and local income taxes. You then earn a Social Security retirement benefit you may elect to take as early as age 62 or, if you wish a higher benefit, then as late as age 70 ½, calculated in part on your lifetime earnings. Your Medicare taxes enable you to enroll in Medicare Part A giving you free basic hospitalization, short-term nursing, and hospice care. You also qualify to pay a monthly premium for Medicare Part B insurance giving you expanded hospitalization, physician, and therapy care, and Medicare Part D prescription-drug coverage. Consult your lawyer if you have any concerns or questions over these laws supporting your retirement. Plan for the best advantages from them to promote your secure retirement.

Audit: Which of the following programs are you planning for in retirement, and on what terms as indicated? (a) Social Security (starting at what age). (b) Defined-benefit pension plan (from what employer and at what benefit amount at what age). (c) Defined-contribution pension plan (through what employer and in what estimated amount at retirement). (d) Medicare Part A. (e) Medicare Part B. (f) Medicare Part D. Consult your lawyer if you have questions or concerns over qualifying for these programs. **Score [___]**

Available Law Services: advising and representing you regarding qualifying for defined-benefit or defined-contribution retirement plans; helping you evaluate and prepare early-withdrawal requests to avoid penalties; representing you to resolve questions over your Social Security retirement benefits; advising you and advocating for your Medicare benefits.

Your Taxes

Federal, state, and local laws tax your earnings. Those taxes are substantial enough, and the penalties for not paying taxes are serious enough, that you should ensure that you comply with these laws. Your employer should be withholding income taxes, unless you are self-employed, in which case you should be setting aside taxes out of your earnings and making the required quarterly payments. Tax withholding, though, does not alone satisfy your obligation. The primary way in which you comply with tax laws is to file accurate annual federal, state, and (in many places) local tax returns that calculate your remaining obligation or refund after withholding. Your failure to file tax returns can result in criminal charges and civil fines and penalties. Tax authorities audit a certain number of returns for accuracy and may pursue criminal charges and assess civil fines and penalties for inaccurate and fraudulent returns. You should ensure that you have made reasonable investigation confirming the accuracy of everything you report on any tax return. Choosing among alternative filing statuses, for instance whether jointly with or separately from a spouse, affects tax rates and obligations. Many different credits, deductions, and exemptions can also make substantial differences in total tax obligations. When you make a gain on the sale of certain investments or earn interest and dividends, you may owe capital-gains tax. States and some locales also impose sales taxes. Individuals and organizations selling goods must collect and remit the sales tax to the state or locale. Some states exempt nonprofit organizations from paying sales taxes on purchases by the organization. You also pay real-property taxes on your residence and other buildings and lands. State laws permit you to challenge the annual property-tax assessment, while laws in some states cap annual increases for your homestead. Consult your lawyer regarding your tax withholding, return, payment, refund, and audit, and for tax planning to manage your tax obligations.

Audit: Determine which of the following federal and state income-tax credits, deductions, and exemptions may apply to you: (a) earned-income credit; (b) home-mortgage deduction; (c) medical-expense deduction; (d) moving-expense deduction; (e) business loss; (f) investment loss; (g) loss carry-forwards; (h) home-office expense; (i) exemptions for certain disability; (j) homestead exemption; (k) charitable deductions. Consult your lawyer about these and other tax issues to ensure that you pay what you owe but do not pay more than you need to pay to meet the law. **Score [___]**

Available Law Services: helping you plan your tax obligations; preparing and amending your tax returns; helping you prepare for and representing you in a tax audit; negotiating, contesting, and appealing tax fines and penalties; challenging annual real-property-tax assessments.

9 Your Property

The things that you own, including housing, vehicles, and personal effects, are important to your welfare and the well-being of your family. The law protects your right to use and enjoy your property but limits those uses while imposing other obligations associated with your use and ownership. The law controls your right to recover for property loss whether through liability actions or insurance, and the right of others to recover when suffering loss because of your use of property. Law supports your development of new property forms both in business and creatively. Law also guides how you dispose of property through charitable giving and estate planning. Consider these and related issues in the following audit sections. Know your property rights, responsibilities, and opportunities, to preserve and promote your family's well-being.

Your Ownership

Your rights of ownership begin with the right to occupy or control your property while you either invite or exclude others from doing so. Whether the property is your home and surrounding land or your vehicle or personal effects, your primary interest is in its exclusive control and use. Criminal and civil laws of trespass, robbery, larceny, theft, conversion, and invasion of privacy ensure your rights of exclusive use and control. For example, some state laws mandate punitive damages when others cut trees or take other resources from your land without your permission. You may share property rights with co-owners or, in the case of real property (buildings and lands), with others through easements for things like sight lines, gaining access to other lands, or maintaining utilities. Laws closely regulate your ownership and use of real property, vehicles, weapons, and certain other property. In general, your uses must not interfere with others, who could have nuisance actions against you if your uses do interfere. Ownership also carries the responsibility to keep your property reasonably safe when you invite use by others that benefit you, and free from or warned about hidden dangerous defects when you permit use by others for their benefit. The law also protects your right to improve and benefit financially from your real property within zoning and other land-use restrictions. Those laws give you opportunities to seek variances to make greater use than the laws on their face allow. Laws closely regulate construction on real property but must leave owners reasonable uses. Laws also regulate and tax the sale, transfer, and recording of title to real property and titling and registration of vehicles. The law of real and personal property is extensive and complex, granting you many rights and benefits while imposing some responsibilities. Consult your lawyer about those laws whenever you have concerns, issues, or opportunities.

Audit: Identify whether you have any issues over ownership, title or registration, possession, control, exclusive use, privacy invasions, interfering use, liability, sale, or transfer of any of the following properties: (a) primary residence; (b) surrounding lands; (c) second home and surrounding lands; (d) neighboring lands; (e) vehicles; (f) boats; (g) campers and trailers; (h) electronic sites, wi-fi, and intranets; (i) tools and equipment; (j) credit and accounts; (k) name, image, or other identity. Consult your lawyer to address those issues. **Score [___]**

Available Law Services: making demands and obtaining orders to prevent trespass or conversion; filing civil actions and seeking criminal-case restitution for stolen property; responding to claims of nuisance; defending you in premises liability actions over injuries on your lands; defending you in liability actions involving use of vehicles, weapons, or other personal property; advocating for changes in or variances from zoning and other land-use restrictions; assisting with your sale and transfer of title to real property and vehicles.

Your Loss

With your property meaning so much to you, you should be able to recover it—or recover for it—in the event of its loss. The law helps protect your property in many ways. In the event of its theft, criminal sentencing laws support orders of restitution requiring the thief to either return the property if it remains within the thief's control or to pay you for all or part of the property's value. If law-enforcement officials are unable or unwilling to help you recover your property, perhaps because of disputes over ownership, then you have a civil right of action in conversion to recover your property from the person who took it or presently has it. Those who buy from thieves do so at their peril. State laws prefer original owners over purchasers from thieves. If your property is buildings or lands, then your private right of action is for an order of possession and to exclude the trespasser. When you and others legitimately dispute ownership, you may file a civil action for a court's declaratory judgment as to your ownership. The court may issue emergency restraining order and preliminary injunction to prevent loss or damage to the property, preserving the status quo until the court is able to decide your dispute fairly. Government officials themselves must ordinarily not take your private property without just compensation except for special circumstances such as under criminal-enterprise forfeiture laws. You have constitutional and statutory rights to recover from government for unlawful takings of your property, including regulatory takings that eliminate your property's value. Finally, the law provides you with the right to recover from others whose carelessness damages or destroys your property. The negligent wrongdoer's liability insurer may owe you the obligation to pay for that loss or damage. Property-insurance contracts and laws are the subject of the next section. Consult your lawyer when you have claims, concerns, or questions over your property loss.

Audit: Identify whether you recently suffered, are suffering, or expect to suffer theft, conversion, interference, encroachment on, damage to, or destruction of any of the following kinds of your property: (a) primary residence; (b) surrounding lands; (c) second home and surrounding lands; (d) vehicles; (e) boats; (f) campers or trailers; (g) software or other electronic or virtual data or property; (h) tools and equipment; (i) securities; (j) financial or other accounts; (k) name, image, or other identity. Consult your lawyer to address those issues or issues on any other real or personal property you own. **Score [___]**

Available Law Services: advocating for you in criminal investigations and at sentencing hearings for restitution of your property; investigating and filing conversion actions to recover your property from thieves and subsequent purchasers; pursuing trespass and declaratory-judgment actions to establish and preserve your property rights; obtaining restraining orders and injunctions to preserve and recover your property; investigating and maintaining condemnation claims against government to recover for loss of your property; maintaining claims in negligence to recover for careless destruction of your property; negotiating with liability insurers for settlement of your property claims.

Your Insurance

Another way that the law helps you control the risk of property loss is through the laws of insurance. Insurance is a contract between you (the insured) and the insurance company (the insurer) that issues the insurance policy. Contract law thus controls in part the obligations of the insurer. You should get the full benefit of the insurance policy's terms. Read your insurance policies for the property that the policies cover, the causes of loss that the policies cover, and the amount and types of benefits that the policies pay to you. By their express terms, property-insurance policies may cover some of your property but not other portions or items of your property, such as highly valuable art or musical instruments that you did not disclose to the insurer that you had. Policies may exclude certain types of loss such as intentional destruction, destruction by undisclosed business use, or destruction by flood. Policies routinely limit the total benefit so that insurers pay only up to the limit amount even when your loss is greater. Policies may also pay for more than just the value of the damaged or destroyed property. They may also pay for loss of use until you are able to repair or replace the property, or pay for other related expenses. You have a private right of action for breach of contract when your property insurer refuses to pay for owing coverage. Courts will construe coverage in your favor and against the insurer when the insurer has written coverage terms ambiguously. Your greater challenge in a civil proceeding may be proving the existence and value of your property before its destruction. Using your smartphone, periodically video-record your personal property to be able later to prove its existence, nature, and extent. Beyond contract law and the civil action you may file to enforce your insurance policy, federal and state laws also regulate insurers through administrative agencies. Those insurance laws and regulations may require insurers to extend coverage beyond the policy's terms. Agencies may even enforce their regulations in ways that help you recover those insurance benefits. Insurance laws and regulations may also increase or ease your recovery if you must pursue a private right of action against your insurer. When applying for property insurance or advocating your claims, you must not misrepresent the extent, condition, or value of your property, the cause or extent of its damage or destruction, or any other material term, or you may lose your insurance, suffer civil judgment in fraud, and face criminal charges. Consult your lawyer with your questions, claims, and concerns of your property-insurance coverage.

Audit: For any of your property that you currently insure, review the policies confirming these particulars: (a) accurate description of the property; (b) current policy period; (c) adequate policy limits to insure its full value; (d) coverage of all reasonably likely causes of loss; (e) no reasonably likely exclusions; (f) all appropriate related benefits such as loss of use. Are you not insuring other property that you should be insuring because you cannot afford to replace it? Consult your lawyer for answers to any of your property-insurance questions or concerns. **Score [___]**

Available Law Services: reviewing your property-insurance policies and coverage and advising you as to their terms; helping you document and submit proof of claim to your property insurer; helping you prepare for your property insurer's examination under oath; representing you in claims against your property insurer; defending you in claims brought against you by your property insurer; referring your property-insurance claims to regulators for enforcement; negotiating settlements of your property-insurance claims.

Your Business

The law helps you treat as valuable property the business that you create through self-employment. You may have regular employment through a company owned by others but operate your own business as a second job on the side, or you may be entirely self-employed. You may even employ others in your business. Businesses obviously have many legal rights, responsibilities, and opportunities. Consider here, though, how law supports your personal interest in your business. You may operate your business as a sole proprietorship, meaning that you are the business. You personally then have the full rights, responsibilities, and liabilities of other businesses. State laws give you the option of forming your business as a partnership with one or more partners, in which case you each have the full rights, responsibilities, and liabilities of the business as partners. Partnerships divide the earnings or losses and assets and debts of the partnership between the partners as the partnership agreement provides or as the state partnership laws provide in the absence of agreement. You may alternatively form your business as a limited-liability company under state laws. As the name implies, the limited-liability-company form ordinarily limits the business's liabilities to the company itself, giving you some protection from those liabilities. You and any other members owning the limited-liability company will pay taxes on the business's earnings just as you would in a partnership. You may alternatively form your business as a corporation under state laws, giving you similar liability protection and additional opportunities to raise capital through public stock offerings regulated by securities laws. Small family owned businesses can grow into large businesses having substantial social and financial value when their owners make proper use of business laws. Consult your lawyer when you have a business to organize and manage.

Audit: If you have self-employment, then determine the following to help you evaluate whether and how to organize your self-employment as a business: (a) how many hours you work in the business each week; (b) your earnings from the business; (c) whether others work in the business with you and, if so, then how many; (d) what ownership you have of the business or share with others; (e) what assets the business owns and their total value; (f) what contracts the business enters into; (g) what risk of liability the business creates; (h) whether the business requires additional capital (investors or loans); (i) whether you wish to convey the business now or at later date. Consult your lawyer about any questions or concerns your evaluation raises and whether to organize your business. **Score [___]**

Available Law Services: advising you on the best business form for your self-employment; drafting a partnership agreement for you and partners; organizing your limited-liability company; forming your corporation; representing your business once formed.

Your Creativity

Beyond your productivity in business, the law also protects your intellectual property and creative works whether or not those works are within your business. Your creative works may have monetary value to you that you wish to retain and promote, or you may simply prefer to restrict use of your creative works to your own use. In many cases, the law gives you the authority to control the use of your creative works. Copyright law protects your original works not when they are simply ideas or concepts but instead when you fix them in a tangible medium of expression. When you author a book, paint a painting, sculpt a sculpture, or create similar original works, you have fixed your ideas in a tangible medium and can copyright those works by so indicating on the work with your name, the year, and the copyright word or symbol. You may also register your copyright to gain additional rights and protections. Trademark laws permit you to register a distinctive word, symbol, or phrase, and in some cases a color or other distinguishing feature, that you use to identify and sell your goods or services. Federal trademark law permits you to you register your mark, while some state laws also support trademark registration. Other state laws may grant some protection from your unregistered usage, particularly when others deliberately use your mark to confuse the public as to the source of goods and services within your market. Federal patent law protects your inventions when they involve an appropriate process, material composition, or improvement, and your invention has utility, novelty, and non-obviousness, and your application adequately describes it. Consult your lawyer about copyright, trademarks, and patents to protect your creative works and intellectual property.

Audit: Identify which of the following original works or inventions you have created that might warrant protection as intellectual property: (a) songs; (b) poems; (c) fiction writing; (d) non-fiction writing; (e) graphic works; (f) audio recordings; (g) video recordings; (h) sculpture or other three-dimensional artwork; (i) words, phrases, or symbols identifying your products; (j) formulas; (k) processes; (l) machines; (m) designs or improvements. Consult your lawyer regarding whether and how to protect these works. **Score [___]**

Available Law Services: helping you identify your intellectual property and create an intellectual-property program; advising you on copyright law; registering your copyrighted works; advising you trademark law; registering your trademarks; advising you on patent law; patenting your inventions and advocating with the Patent Office; helping you license your intellectual property; representing you in actions against others who violate your intellectual-property rights.

Your Giving

The law not only affects your acquiring, owning, and enjoying property but also giving it away. Under ordinary circumstances, you may of course relinquish things that you own as you wish, whether loaning, selling, or bartering them, or giving them away. Federal law ordinarily imposes a gift tax on the donor when the gift's value (whether cash or other property) exceeds $14,000 to any individual in one year. Together, you and your spouse may give up to $28,000 to one individual in one year without paying the federal gift tax. Federal law does not tax your gifts to your spouse, tuition or medical expense that you pay for another, or gifts to charities that the federal government has recognized. Federal law permits individuals who itemize their income-tax deductions to deduct from their taxable income the value of their qualifying charitable donations. You may, in other words, get a tax break for making charitable contributions. You do not get a tax break for contributing your services to a charity, even when you are able to put monetary values on your services. To be deductible, your contribution must be of cash or tangible items for which you can establish a fair market value. You must reduce your contribution amount by any tangible item of value that you receive in return for the contribution, such as a meal or gift at a fundraiser. The federal law of foundations enables you or your family to dedicate large sums to charity while continuing to advise the granting of those funds to specific organizations and activities you find worthy of your charity. Many individuals also gather with others to form their own charitable organizations to which they and others can contribute property and services. Consult your lawyer if you have questions about contributing tax-deductible sums to charity or taxable amounts to others, or wish to form a charity or foundation.

Audit: Identify which of the following gifts you have made in the recent past or anticipate making in the near future: (a) gifts of more than $14,000 in one year to any individual; (b) gifts of non-cash property approaching or exceeding $14,000 in value; (c) charitable gifts of any amount that you intend to deduct from your income for tax purposes; (d) contributions to social-welfare organizations for issue advocacy; (e) contributions to political candidates; (f) contributions to any organization for political purposes. Consult your lawyer if you have questions or concerns about the taxation, tax deductibility, appraisal, documentation and proof, or procedure for any of these gifts or contributions. **Score [___]**

Available Law Services: advising you on gift-tax limits; documenting and appraising your taxable gifts, and completing your gift-tax returns; confirming the charitable status of organizations to which you wish to contribute tax-deductible sums; documenting and appraising your charitable contributions; forming and advising your charitable organization; forming and advising your foundation.

Your Estate

Law has a lot to do with your property's disposition after your death. Your property that you do not give away during your life ordinarily becomes a part of your estate after your death. You may decide to hold some property (particularly your residence or other real property but possibly also savings, retirement, or other accounts) jointly with your spouse or with others in a form that grants them rights of survivorship. With the property title properly so providing, your joint interest would then dissolve on your death, meaning that full ownership would pass to the other without your joint interest becoming part of your estate. You may also designate beneficiaries and secondary beneficiaries on life insurance, annuities, and other interests and accounts such that they pass straight to those persons without passing through your estate. You may also form a trust into which some or all of your assets pass on your death, providing in the trust document for the control and disposition of those funds. Otherwise, your estate will collect, manage, and dispose of your property after your death, subject to the claims of creditors and estate-administration expenses. You get to direct the disposition that your estate makes of your property if you execute a will meeting the requirements of state law. You may direct your property to your spouse, children, grandchildren, friends, or charities as you see fit, although state laws give your spouse certain rights if your will fails to provide for your spouse and may give certain rights to your children particularly if born after your will. State law requires that you be competent and not unduly influenced or defrauded by others when executing or changing your will. If you do not execute a valid will, then your estate disposes of your property according to the presumptions that state laws provide, typically dividing property among your spouse, children, and other commonly recognized and natural heirs. Federal and state law tax estates, and courts may charge fees for estate administration. Planning your estate may secure your property for your family or charities while saving taxes and expenses. Consult your lawyer regarding your estate plan.

Audit: Confirm how you have provided after your death for the following: (a) your spouse; (b) minor children; (c) adult children; (d) grandchildren; (e) parents; (f) siblings; (g) other relatives close to you; (h) other dependents; (i) close friends; (j) charities; (k) religious organizations; (l) community foundations; (m) business partners. Then confirm how you have provided for the disposition after your death of the following types of property that you may own: (a) residence; (b) second residence; (c) vehicles; (d) business interests; (e) retirement accounts; (f) other brokerage accounts; (g) savings accounts; (h) savings bonds; (i) certificates of deposit; (j) life insurance; (k) valuable or sentimental art or jewelry; (l) sports and recreational equipment; (m) other personal effects; (n) copyrights, patents, and other intellectual property. Consult your lawyer to provide for these persons and entities, and your disposition of these properties. **Score [___]**

Available Law Services: advising you on your estate plan; reviewing and revising your deeds, titles, accounts, and interests for rights of survivorship; drafting, reviewing, and revising your will; drafting, reviewing, and revising your trust; probating your estate.

10 Your Freedom

The rule of law guarantees you freedoms. Others have paid preciously in order that you have the right and opportunity to use them. Consider whether you are enjoying these freedoms to the fullest extent. Consider your freedoms of religion, speech, and association, all fundamental rights the U.S. Constitution enshrines in its First Amendment. Exercise these freedoms fully while respecting the rights of others to do likewise. We are healthiest when we do so. The law grants you these and other fundamental rights as privileges of your U.S. citizenship. Know your rights and responsibilities as a citizen, and exercise them fully to ensure our continued freedom. If you or your family members are not citizens, then know that the law nonetheless guarantees non-citizens fundamental rights. The law even grants asylum and other protections to the undocumented alien, while further granting constitutional protections to the arrestee and prisoner. Consider the following sections elaborating these freedoms.

Your Religion

The Founders' decision to make freedom of religion the first right in the First Amendment of the Bill of Rights was no coincidence. Federal and state constitutions and laws ensure that you have the right and opportunity to use that most fundamental of all rights, that you pursue your religion fully and freely. The law enables you to be more than a nominal adherent. You may read, quote, and rely on religious scripture, attend and participate in religious services, study, learn, and teach religious doctrine, serve in religious missions, give to and receive from religious charities, and pray prayers and sing songs of faith. You would have none of these opportunities without the rule of law. Leaders in other countries without the rule of law ban, persecute, imprison, starve, torture, condemn, and kill peace-loving traditional religious adherents. To preserve your fullest religious freedom, the law prohibits government from establishing religion. You get to choose, not the government. While the First Amendment expressly restricts Congress from establishing or interfering with the free exercise of religion, the Fourteenth Amendment extends that protection to prohibit similar actions by state and local government. Federal and state religious-freedom acts prohibit even generally neutral laws that nonetheless substantially burden your freedom of religion, with certain exceptions. Federal statute creates a private right of action to enjoin government from interfering with your religious practices and to hold it liable in damages for your harm. Federal and state anti-discrimination laws ensure that your religion does not keep you from gaining and holding employment, or enjoying public services and accommodations. Consult your lawyer if government is interfering with your free exercise of religion.

Audit: Do you face any interference with your free exercise of religion in the nature of any of the following examples? (a) Zoning officials refusing variances for houses of worship. (b) Inspectors enforcing building codes to prevent religious uses. (c) Local officials refusing to allow religious studies or meetings in homes. (d) Local officials refusing to allow street preaching. (e) Local officials requiring licenses for door-to-door religious workers. (f) Schoolteachers refusing to allow children to sing worship songs, read scripture, or speak about religion. (g) Employers refusing to accommodate religious clothing, symbols, worship, or prayer. (h) Employers refusing to hire because of religion. (i) Hotels, restaurants, and other places of public service and accommodation refusing service because of your religion. (j) Laws prohibiting use of peyote or other substances in religious practices. Consult your lawyer for advice and protection if you face any of these issues. **Score [___]**

Available Law Services: research and advice on protecting your religious practices; notices to and negotiation with public officials to end interference with your religious practices; representing you in claims against government agencies and officials to end interference with your religious practices and for damages; representing you in claims against employers and places of public service and accommodation to end religious discrimination against you and recover damages.

Your Speech

The First and Fourteenth Amendments also protect your free speech and freedom of association from government interference. Your free speech involves your right to express yourself as you wish on political and public issues, as to public figures, and artistically and in other ways. Free-speech rights even protect you in some cases from defamation actions as long as you are not reckless as to the truth or falsity of your statements. Your freedom of association, coming from the First Amendment's rights to assemble and petition the government, protect you against government interference when gathering with others to discuss and pursue political, economic, religious, cultural, or other matters. While officials may make reasonable content-neutral safety restrictions on the time, place, and manner of public speech and assemblies, federal, state, and local government should not be passing laws, rules, or regulations, requiring licenses or other permission, or taking enforcement actions based on the content of your speech or that unduly abridge these rights without compelling justification. Federal law creates a private civil right of action for damages and injunctions when government officials interfere with these rights. You may sue to preserve these rights. Federal, state, and local civil-rights laws extend these protections to places of public service and accommodation, meaning that in many cases, businesses may not refuse you service because of your speech, memberships, and associations. Free-speech and freedom-of-association rights extend to protecting your public employment. If you work for government, then your employer should not be using your free speech or your associations to affect adversely your employment. You may generally, for instance, support the political candidate or cause you wish, without your public employer retaliating against you. The law may also entitle you to notice and hearing before demotion or termination from your public employment. Consult your lawyer if you face official restrictions on your speech or association, or suffer adverse public-employment actions.

Audit: Do you face any interference with your free-speech or freedom-of-association rights in the nature of the following examples? (a) Denied a parade license. (b) Refused use of public facilities. (c) Required to disclose memberships. (d) Refused public benefit. (e) Refused public service or accommodation. (f) Fired from or demoted in public employment. Consult your lawyer for assistance with these or similar free-speech and freedom-of-association rights. **Score [___]**

Available Law Services: researching and advising you on your rights of free speech and freedom of association; notifying and negotiating with public officials for the free exercise of your rights; representing you in challenges to laws and licenses interfering with your free speech and association; defending you in enforcement actions taken on the basis of your free speech and associations; advising you regarding your public-employment rights of free speech and association; representing you in actions involving your public employment; representing you in claims against places of public service and accommodation for discrimination against you based on your free speech and association.

Your Citizenship

The law recognizes and values your citizenship. Citizenship depends on your birth within the United States or in some cases certain U.S. territories or possessions, or your birth to a U.S.-citizen parent and you meet other requirements. You may alternatively apply after birth for citizenship through a statutory naturalization process. Naturalization ordinarily requires that you pass an English-language and civics test. Your citizenship and its proper documentation by passport or otherwise can be critical to your ability to return to the United States from foreign countries. Entry after exit is just one of many rights and privileges of citizenship, which include all protections of citizens under the U.S. Constitution. Citizens have additional rights beyond the rights of non-citizens and undocumented aliens, for example, to vote for public officials, accept certain federal employment, and run for certain public office. Lawful resident aliens who have a documented status to remain in the United States without having U.S. citizenship may have certain constitutional protections without having these additional special citizenship rights. Undocumented aliens who are neither citizens or lawful resident aliens retain some constitutional rights but under federal law lose their opportunity to work lawfully within the United States, among other significant disadvantages. Citizenship rights come with responsibilities to defend the Constitution, defend the country if called upon, serve on juries, pay taxes, obey the law, respect the rights of others, and, more broadly, participate in the democratic process. You may in certain cases have dual citizenship, particularly when you acquire a foreign citizenship automatically rather than by application, or when naturalized as a U.S. citizen while keeping your foreign citizenship if that foreign

111

law allows it. The law allows renunciation of your citizenship before a U.S. consular officer in a foreign country.

Audit: Confirm the following: (a) that you are a U.S. citizen or lawful resident alien within the United States; (b) that you have a current U.S. passport or current visa proving your lawful status; (c) that you have the status and documentation to leave and re-enter the United States without difficulty. If you have any concerns or questions over these issues, or you have a family member who does, then consult your lawyer about your citizenship or lawful status in the United States. **Score [___]**

Available Law Services: assisting you with your citizenship application; advising you as to dual citizenship; helping you obtain a U.S. passport or the documentation necessary for a U.S. passport; helping you or your relatives obtain visas; representing you in deportation or other immigration proceedings; advising you as to renunciation of citizenship.

Your Asylum

Even when you do not have citizenship or your citizenship is limited, the law provides substantial protections for you. Immigrants who enter the United States without lawful documentation, commonly called illegal aliens, gain basic constitutional protections and, with it, other legal rights. As an illegal alien, you gain due process rights, meaning that the government not deny your life, liberty, or property without fair notice and hearing. You also gain equal protection rights, meaning that you have the same access to public education and other services that citizens and documented aliens enjoy. You may be subject to detention and deportation after hearing but have other opportunities within federal immigration laws and practices to remain in the country. Asylum is an option for those who entered the country illegally for haven from persecution in their home country due to their race, religion, nationality, social-group membership, or political opinion. Applying for asylum gives you a temporary status for the year or more that process takes. If you establish your right to asylum, then after one year you may apply for a green card for permanent residency, putting you on a path to citizenship. Even when you have citizenship but have lost your freedom, the law continues to provide you protections. On arrest and detention, you have the right to remain silent, consult your lawyer, and appear before a judge usually within 48 hours to hear the charges against you, enter a plea, and schedule a bail hearing. During incarceration, the U.S. Constitution protects prisoners from cruel and unusual punishment, ensuring that those who are incarcerated receive adequate food, drink, exercise, air, and medical care. Prisoners have access to law materials, the courts, and their lawyer to ensure these rights and the integrity of the process that resulted in their incarceration. The law protects even the most vulnerable.

Audit: Identify any of the following freedom issues that you or your family members face, as undocumented aliens, arrestees, or prisoners: (a) rights to public school or other services; (b) deportation proceedings; (c) foreign persecution; (d) refugee status; (e) arrest and detention; (f) bail or bond for release; (g) jail or prison conditions affecting health; (h) medical care while incarcerated. Consult your lawyer regarding any of these freedom issues. **Score [___]**

Available Law Services: representing the undocumented alien regarding due process and equal protection rights; representing you or family members in deportation proceedings; helping you or family members apply for asylum; advising you when arrested; representing you at arraignment, preliminary examination, and bail hearing; representing you or your family members regarding conditions of incarceration.

Your Information

One final area in which you have a personal interest, that promotes your liberty, and with which the law helps you is information. Information is power. Federal and state Freedom of Information Acts require the government to disclose to you public records on your request. Those acts exempt certain records such as records of ongoing law-enforcement investigations and records having to do with national or local security. The acts also permit the government to charge you reasonable costs for searching for and copying the records. Yet your ability to discover information that the government has collected about you, your family, your business, and the activities of others can be a powerful tool. You may first discover and ensure that the information about you is accurate, communicating with public officials to challenge and correct those inaccuracies. You may also use public records for your business, security, investing, or other social, political, recreational, and economic activities. The government is a vast repository of public, private, and commercial information. Federal and state information acts have proven powerful tools in ensuring our continued freedom while expanding our opportunities. Consult your lawyer for help in using information acts for any lawful purpose.

Audit: Identify any of the following public records in which you may have a personal, political, social, recreational, economic, or other interest: (a) your criminal history; (b) your civil or family court records; (c) your real-estate-tax and assessment records; (d) your building-inspection records; (e) police reports of accidents and other events in which you were involved; (f) records of fire, sewer, power, cable, drain, or other public services and utilities for your home; (g) records and reports involving others in your neighborhood potentially affecting the safety of your family; (h) records of home sales in your neighborhood affecting your property value; (i) records of the proceedings of local public bodies on actions affecting you; (j) records of public officials regulating your property or business; (k) names, addresses, and other contact information for potential customers of your business; (l) maps and photographs of lands; (m) building or facility diagrams. Consult your lawyer for assistance with obtaining any of this information or similar information. **Score [___]**

Available Law Services: advising you as to which public records you may obtain under federal and state information acts; helping you make information-act requests; representing you in information-act lawsuits to obtain public records.

Conclusion

Your Trust

I think often of my first client, the unusual trust that he placed in law, and the success his confidence brought him. When I think of the trust that I have seen so many others put in law with similar results, the power of law to improve lives becomes all the more obvious. My services to my first client were in no sense special or distinct. I was then a brand new lawyer. What was unusual was his faith in the law, which was then greater than my own, even though I was the lawyer. My first client and then many others who followed taught me to have the faith in law that is law's due. May you share that faith as I have learned to share that faith, and may your faith bless you richly as you learn to draw on the power and purpose of law. You have many lesser things in which you could place your trust, not the least of which would be your own judgment uninformed by the law's wisdom of the ages. Let your lawyer be your confidant, conscience, and guide.

About the Author

Nelson Miller is a professor and associate dean at Thomas M. Cooley Law School. Before joining Cooley, Dean Miller practiced civil litigation for 16 years in a small-firm setting, representing individuals, corporations, agencies, and public and private universities. He has published 22 books and dozens of book chapters and articles on law and law practice. The State Bar of Michigan recognized Dean Miller with the John W. Cummiskey Award for pro-bono service. He earned his law degree at the University of Michigan before joining the firm that later became Fajen and Miller, PLLC, his practice base before moving full-time into law teaching.

CPSIA information can be obtained
at www.ICGtesting.com
Printed in the USA
BVOW06s1454200917
495425BV00011B/96/P